Explaining Your Faith

Explaining Your Faith

Alister McGrath

Baker Books

A Division of Baker Book House Co.
Grand Rapids, Michigan 49516

© 1988, 1995 by Alister McGrath

Published by Baker Books
a division of Baker Book House Company
P.O. Box 6287, Grand Rapids, MI 49516-6287

Paperback edition published 1996

Previously published in Great Britain by Inter-Varsity Press

Printed in the United States of America

Library of Congress Cataloging-in-Publication Data

McGrath, Alister E., 1953–
    Explaining your faith / Alister McGrath.
      p. cm.
    Rev. ed. of: Explaining your faith without losing your
friends. c1989.
    Includes bibliographical references.
    ISBN 0-8010-5728-0
    1. Apologetics—20th century. 2. College students—
Religious life. I. McGrath, Alister E., 1953– Explaining your
faith without losing your friends. II. Title.
BT1102.M43 1996
239—dc20   96-9239

Contents

Foreword

If Christianity is so wonderful, why isn't everyone a Christian? One of the reasons is that we often explain the gospel so badly that people lose interest in it. Many Christians take little trouble to explain what the gospel is all about. They assume that there is no point in wasting valuable time in explaining what ought to be obvious to everyone. Yet what holds many people back from becoming Christians is a genuine lack of understanding of what Christianity is all about, or why it could have any relevance to their lives. Someone needs to take time to explain it.

Yet many Christians have another problem at this point. They themselves are not sure what Christianity has to say, or how they could best help someone to appreciate its great attraction. Because they have never thought their faith through for themselves, they don't stand a chance of helping someone who is genuinely interested in learning more about the gospel to travel the final stages of the road that leads to faith. Christians who understand their faith are far better evangelists than those who do not. This little book will help you understand more about the gospel and cope with the questions and problems that your friends will bring to you.

This book had its origins back in 1987 as a series of four talks given to students at Oxford University in preparation for a mission to their university. The lectures were meant to help students deal with some of the questions and objections which their friends might have concerning Christianity. However, the questions and issues that students face have changed considerably over the last few years, and it was clear that there was a real need to expand and revise this book in their light. Above all, there are new cultural pressures which are proving hostile to the gospel, and which students on university campuses are experiencing with particular force. This expanded edition will be of use to a new generation of Christian students as they explain and defend their faith on the university campuses of the world.

In revising the text, I have drawn on my experience of sharing and explaining the Christian faith at university campuses in North America and Australia. I am especially grateful to students at McGill University (Montreal), Drew University (Madison, New Jersey), Wheaton College (Illinois), and the universities of British Columbia, Melbourne, New South Wales and Sydney for comments and guidance.

Alister McGrath
Regent College
Vancouver, May 1994

How to use this book

'Always be prepared to give an answer to everyone who asks you to give the reason for the hope that you have' (1 Peter 3:15).

This book is meant to help you explain and defend Christianity to your friends. It isn't an evangelism manual. It isn't a theological textbook. It is just meant to help you explain the great attraction of the gospel, and deal with some of the difficulties which people – especially students! – genuinely feel when they are considering the claims of Christianity. Obviously there isn't space enough to deal with all the difficulties people have with the gospel, just as there isn't space enough to give very detailed replies to these. So what you will find is an outline of what seem to be the most common problems and objections, with suggestions of what you might say in response to them, and recommended reading to allow you to follow up any points in further detail. The ideas and approaches set out here have been tried out on university campuses in North America, Australia and Great Britain, and adapted in the light of student response. You can therefore be confident that they are worth taking seriously. You may need to adapt them for your own needs, or supplement them on the basis of other books recommended in the text.

The arrangement of the book is quite simple. It is divided into three parts, each dealing with a different aspect of presenting and defending the gospel as effectively as possible. The first part deals with things that need to be sorted out before you will be able to explain the content of the gospel and allow your friends to appreciate the great joy and excitement which it brings. The second part deals with four groups of difficulties that people have about the Christian faith. You will find that mastering these sections will help you gain increased confidence in your own faith, as well as explain it to others! Finally, the third part deals with a series of difficulties raised for the gospel through recent cultural pressures, such as the rise of pluralism. At the end there is a list of books suggested for further reading, in case you would like to take some issues further, either on your own or with your friends.

1

Introduction

Why should Christians want to evangelize in the first place? Many people are convinced that the only reason that Christians try to persuade their friends to accept the gospel is because they are like native American warriors, anxious to add one more scalp to their collections. The popular idea, which has an especially wide appeal on university campuses, is that evangelism is like some kind of brainwashing or imperialist crusading, aimed at getting everyone to conform to Christian ideas.

Yet they have missed out on something here. When people become Christians, as they still do in large numbers, they discover something – or, better, some*one* – who transforms their lives. They are aware of a new sense of peace, joy and purpose in their lives. It is only natural that they should want to tell their friends about it. After all, one of the most powerful human instincts is the desire to share the good things of life! Christians are people who have discovered something which they cannot keep to themselves. They want to share it! And that is why they evangelize.

Evangelism is like one beggar telling another where to find bread. For Christians, the 'bread of life' is none other than Jesus Christ himself. It is Jesus Christ who meets the real and deep spiritual hunger of humankind. It is to him that Christians point as the source and ground of their faith. To come to Jesus Christ is to discover a whole new dimension to life. It is to come to life. It is to embrace him

11

as our Lord and Saviour. And somehow, nothing seems quite the same again afterwards.

So it's perhaps not surprising that many Christians find it difficult to understand the difficulties their non-Christian friends have with Christianity. Your life, like human history, may be divided into two parts: before Christ and after Christ. And many Christians find it very difficult to think themselves back into a situation where they weren't Christians.

Yet if you want to explain the relevance and excitement of Christianity to your non-Christian friends, you will have to try and think yourself into their situation. For you, Christianity is like bread to a starving beggar – a lifesaver. Yet they may see it in a very different light. What you now see as bread, they may see as poison – perhaps a rather unpleasant way of committing intellectual suicide! You must remember that Christianity looks very different from the inside looking out than it does from the outside looking in.

To you, Christianity is exciting, vital and relevant. But your friends may not see it like that. To them, it may appear as something dull and irrelevant. You may offer them the bread of life – but they may tell you that they aren't hungry. Even before you can begin to show how Christianity meets the spiritual hunger of men and women, you may find yourself having to prove that there *is* a spiritual hunger in the first place! Again, you may find yourself overwhelmed by the knowledge that God has graciously forgiven your sins in Jesus' name – but your friends may feel that they haven't any sins which need forgiving in the first place! 'Anyway,' they might ask, 'what is sin?'

Again, in the light of your encounter with the living God you may recognize that the intellectual obstacles to belief in God aren't really very important. After all, when you have encountered the living God, it's very difficult to understand why anyone *doesn't* believe in him! But your friends will see these difficulties as being much more serious. They haven't had the experience which shows these difficulties in their proper light. For them, belief in God may be like believing in Santa Claus or fairies – something which is at best improbable, and at worst totally ludicrous.

From the outside looking in

Christianity often seems strange when viewed from the outside. Many non-believers tend to think of their Christian friends as being just a little weird. They may like them a lot, yet have problems understanding why they want to do some things, such as reading the Bible or going to church. Why do they behave like this? Why do they want to read their Bibles? Why do they want to sing hymns and songs about God and Jesus? Why should they want to pray? It is difficult for a non-Christian to work out what's going on. An example may help bring this out.

Let's suppose that you have a friend – let's call him Pete. One day Pete starts behaving strangely. He starts wanting to spend time with a girl called Ann. He starts writing lots of long and apparently pointless letters to her. He starts sending her flowers. He seems preoccupied. In short: he's fallen in love with Ann. Now to those who have never fallen in love, his behaviour seems eccentric. Why should he want to do these apparently idiotic things? But to those who have shared the experience of falling in love, his behaviour is perfectly reasonable.

Now those who wonder why Christians want to spend time praying to God, or worshipping him, or reading the Bible, are rather like people who have never fallen in love trying to figure out what Pete was doing. They haven't shared the *experience* which makes people *want* to do these things! Once they have that experience themselves, of course, they can understand why Christians want to do these things. They just come naturally.

In a way, trying to explain Christianity to a non-Christian is rather like trying to explain falling in love to someone who's never had that experience. You could try and explain it in rather academic terms – like what it is that Christians believe. Yet this doesn't really convey the excitement of Christian faith, any more than a definition of 'falling in love' can express what that really feels like!

Your non-Christian friends may try to invalidate your experience and behaviour: 'He's got religion,' or 'She's fallen in with the Jesus crowd.' They feel threatened by it – it's not something they can really understand. And so they try to dismiss it. But don't let this discourage you. Remember the famous words of the great German writer Goethe: 'We are used to the fact that people make fun of things which they don't understand.' Ridiculing your experience doesn't *invalidate* it – any more than ridiculing Pete would invalidate the fact that he'd fallen in love with Ann!

The basic point you need to remember is this. To be of real help to your friends as they wrestle with Christianity, you must try and think yourself into their situation. You must empathize with them, to use the jargon. It isn't particularly helpful to adopt a 'take it or leave it' attitude. You may find that you have to take some time and trouble trying to explain ideas which are obvious to you, but which your friends seem to have enormous difficulty in grasping.

This book is written to help you do this. It aims to help you explain Christianity to your friends. There is an area of Christian theology known as 'apologetics'. The Greek word *apologia* basically means 'an explanation' or 'a defence'. It is used three times in the New Testament

14

to refer to 'giving a defence of the gospel' (Philippians 1:7, 16; 1 Peter 3:15). 'Apologetics' is about defending the gospel. In many ways, this book can be regarded as a first-step introduction to 'Christian apologetics'.

So what is the difference between apologetics and evangelism? A simple illustration, based on some of the New Testament parables, will make the distinction clear. Jesus often compared the gospel to a banquet, or some kind of great party. Try to imagine two different approaches to that party. The first approach stresses that there really is a party, explains why it is going to be great fun, and reflects on the great time that everyone is going to have. The second approach issues an invitation to that party. It says: 'You're invited.' It asks: 'Are you going to come?'

Apologetics is about affirming the truth and the attraction of the gospel. Evangelism is about issuing a personal invitation to come to faith, and become a Christian. So apologetics is like a kind of pre-evangelism. It prepares the way for that invitation to be issued, by helping people to understand what Christianity is about, and why it is so attractive and meaningful. Then the way is clear for the next stage: an invitation or challenge can be laid down.

Many books have been written on the subject of evangelism. This one is primarily about apologetics. In other words, it aims to help you understand how best to explain the attraction of the Christian gospel to your friends, and to respond to some of the questions and difficulties which they may have.

I'm no good at evangelism

At this point, however, you may find yourself thinking, 'Evangelism isn't for me. I'd be no good at it.' Actually, this is the best place to start. It's good to recognize your personal inadequacy – but you need to move on, and see that this isn't quite as important as you think.

You need to recognize both your personal inadequacy, and the irrelevance of this inadequacy to evangelism. It is natural to think that the really effective communicators of the gospel are high-powered, competent and confident. But how many of us are like that? Most of us have enough insight to realize how inadequate we are!

However, the New Testament makes it abundantly clear that God's power works through human weakness (*e.g.* see 1 Corinthians 2:3-5; 2 Corinthians 4:7; 12:7-10). The cross of Jesus Christ – something which the world then thought was (and still thinks is) weak and foolish – is a symbol of the Christian realization that God works through weakness. It isn't what we are that matters – it's what we let God do with us that really counts. Two important points may be made here.

1. Acknowledging our own weakness and inadequacy is actually the first step in turning to God, to ask him for power, strength and wisdom. By recognizing how weak we are, we find it easier to turn to God and claim his strength. After all, it is God's gospel, given and entrusted to us – and we need to learn to rely upon him as we proclaim his gospel in his world. Self-confidence and self-reliance are seriously out of place in the Christian life: the only real ground of confidence is God (1 Corinthians 1:31; 3:21). Prayer is thus both an acknowledgment of our own inadequacy and God's ability to meet our needs.

2. Acknowledging our weakness reminds us of something it is very easy to overlook – that Christianity is not based upon human wisdom, but upon the power of God (see 1 Corinthians 2:3-5). Christianity doesn't make its appeal to some sort of intellectual élite. It isn't based upon contemporary academic wisdom, which is outdated in decades rather than centuries. Anyone who has studied

the history of ideas is aware of just how quickly ideas go out of fashion. They are abandoned, rather than refuted. Underlying the gospel is something which cannot go out of date – the power of God.

The gospel proclaims that the human problem is basically the same today as it always has been – selfish human nature, existing in a sinful fallen world. And the gospel does not merely diagnose this situation, but offers a remedy. So long as men and women seek after truth, the gospel proclamation that Jesus Christ is 'the way, the truth and the life' (John 14:6) will remain a challenge to human concepts of wisdom. So long as human beings walk the face of this earth, knowing that they must die, the gospel proclamation of eternal life will continue to be relevant.

We have not been entrusted with some sort of intellectual or spiritual consumer product with a shelf-life of a few centuries, but with the transforming and creative power of God at work in his world. The gospel will not and cannot go out of date! The gospel is about the living God, who comes to us in Jesus Christ and makes himself available for us. It is especially important for students to grasp this point: they will not be committing themselves to some system of belief which will go out of date within a decade. The gospel has stood the twin tests of time and experience for two thousand years, without giving any indication of being 'irrelevant' or 'outdated' yet!

So if you feel inadequate – don't worry! All of us are inadequate. By recognizing your inadequacy, you will be all the more likely to trust in God, and not yourself. By recognizing our weakness and lack of wisdom, we turn to God, in order to receive his strength and wisdom. God uses us – but, in the end, he doesn't depend upon us. The graveyards of the world are packed full of people who thought that Christianity depended upon them – but the grave couldn't hold the one upon whom Christianity

17

really depends: the risen Christ. And it is by claiming his power and presence, and by pointing people to him, that we best serve him.

Explaining what Christianity really is

Most people have very confused understandings of what Christianity is about! They don't reject Christianity because they have given it careful consideration and decided that it is wrong. In most cases, they encounter a caricature of Christianity, and reject that instead.

In fact, if I could give a personal testimony at this point, one of the things which prejudiced me strongly against Christianity as a young man was a serious misunderstanding of what it was all about. I grew up in Northern Ireland, noted for its religious tensions, back in the 1960s. It was a time when young people across the Western world were rejecting Christianity in favour of political solutions (such as Marxism) to the world's problems. I became a Marxist while at high school, and turned my back on the Christian faith. I was told that it was just the 'narcotic of the people'. I knew little about Christianity, despite attending a very religious high school. All I knew was that, whatever it was, I didn't want it. It was an irrelevance. And so I rejected something I did not know or understand, on the basis of what other people said about it – other people, it turned out, who knew as little about it as I did.

Then I went to Oxford University as a student. I began to hear people explaining what Christianity was for the first time. I began to realize what it was all about. It bore virtually no relation to the dull and tedious stereotype which I had uncritically absorbed. I thought Christianity was all about believing certain things to be true, and having a really boring life as a result. Nobody had told me about the joy and delight of knowing a risen

Saviour and Lord, and being given the hope of eternal life! I realized that I had rejected a caricature, and missed out on the reality. I soon put that one right!

The first rule to remember is this: *to explain Christianity is to defend Christianity*. Don't worry if your friends seem to have the most unlikely ideas about what Christianity is like! Slowly, you can begin to remove these obstacles to faith by explaining what Christianity is really like.

But before you can explain what Christianity is like, you need to have given the matter some thought yourself! Many Christians pay surprisingly little attention to the content of their faith. They concentrate upon experiencing God through prayer, Bible-reading and worship. Now this is no bad thing! But it does mean that you neglect an aspect of being a Christian which is important in evangelism of any sort – being able to explain what Christians believe, and why. There are a number of books readily available which explain clearly and simply what Christians believe (and why!), noted at the end of this book. Try to read some of them.

The remainder of this book, however, is written with this need in mind. It aims to provide a simple, readable and intelligible account of what Christians believe (and why they believe it) in a number of key areas – areas which keep coming up in student discussions. I hope that this will help you understand your own faith better, as well as help you to explain and defend it as you talk to your non-Christian friends.

Yet an important part of explaining our faith relates to helping people appreciate how genuinely attractive the gospel is. All too often, people have little idea of the sheer joy and delight of Christianity. In the following chapter, we will begin to explore ways of communicating this joy.

Part 1

Setting the Scene

2

The attraction of the gospel

Christianity has a bad public-relations problem on its hands. Its popular image, nourished by nineteenth-century stereotypes and twentieth-century prejudice, is that of a dull and tedious set of regulations, which at best stops you having any fun, and at worst oppresses people. There is no need to feel depressed about this. It just means that we need to make sure that we deploy every resource that God has put at our disposal as we set out the case for the Christian faith.

In his *First and Second Things*, C. S. Lewis spoke of the value of 'creating an intellectual (and imaginative) climate favourable to Christianity . . . If the intellectual climate is such that, when a man comes to a crisis at which he must either accept or reject Christ, his reason and imagination are not on the wrong side, then his conflict will be fought out under favourable conditions.' Think of yourself as helping to create this 'intellectual climate favourable to Christianity'. One way of doing this is by enabling people to appreciate the full attraction of the gospel, perhaps for the very first time.

Understand the human need
We must learn to see humanity from the standpoint of the gospel, and appreciate the hopelessness of its situation.

Only by doing so can we realize the full potential of the good news of Jesus Christ, and the ways in which we can best present the gospel to our friends. Taking time to reflect on the Christian understanding of fallen human nature is an essential first step in appreciating why the gospel is indeed such good news.

The gospel portrays humanity as lost, and cut off from authentic life on account of its sin. Sin alienates people from God. It prevents them from coming to know him in all his fullness. It gets in the way of the true goal of human nature, which is to 'glorify God and to enjoy him for ever' (*Westminster Shorter Catechism*). Humanity has been created by God for the purpose of fellowship with God, and has rebelled against him. Yet it feels the pain of his absence. 'You have made us for yourself, and our heart is restless until it finds its rest in you' (Augustine of Hippo). In what follows, we shall use six images, each of which is thoroughly grounded in Scripture, as a way of presenting the human situation without fellowship with God.

Sinful humanity is *hungry*, longing for food which will really satisfy and endure, yet often contenting itself with the latest fast-food novelty, which seems to end up making that hunger even worse. It is *thirsty*, and attempts to quench that thirst with all kinds of things, whether Eastern religions or secular materialism. It is *empty*, and tries to fill the yawning gap in the heart of its nature with anything and everything, only to discover that nothing seems to fit the gap inside it. It is *lonely*, longing for friendship and company, yet finding that human relationships never seem really to solve the problem. It is *hopeless*, as it has nothing to say in the face of death. Knowing this, it tries to deny the reality of death, or take refuge in the hope that death will be something that happens to someone else. And it is *lost*, like a flock of sheep wandering aimlessly across the landscape, looking for food and not sure where to find it.

Many other ways of illuminating the human situation could be noted. For example, it is guilty in the face of a righteous and holy judge. It is soiled and stained, and in need of cleansing and purification. The six noted above have been selected because they are felt with especial force in modern Western culture, which is the context in which the ideas of this book are likely to be used. For example, a depressingly large number of students are known to commit suicide. Why? Why should young people, poised to enter into the fullness of adult life, want to destroy themselves? The answer in a large number of cases is as clear as it is saddening: there is no hope for the future. And lacking any sense of hope, meaning or purpose, they end their young lives.

Christians owe it to people like that to make sure that the good news of the gospel is heard. This world needs hope. The gospel offers no false hope, but a hope which is grounded in the life, death and resurrection of Jesus Christ. It has not been invented with these needs in mind. It is grounded in God himself, who created us and knows us.

Having explored the human need, we can now develop biblically-grounded strategies for ensuring that the gospel is heard for all its worth by our audiences.

Explain the gospel message

One of the most important skills you need to develop is that of identifying the aspect of the gospel which is going to be of greatest importance to your friend. You can rest assured that, by doing this, you are not reducing the gospel to this one aspect! All you are doing is working out which of the many facets of the gospel will be of particular relevance to their situation. It's like the thin end of a wedge; once part of the gospel has gained an entry, the rest will follow. But you need to get your foot in the door first. This means that you need to know something about the gospel, and something about your friends.

You'll need to be able to have a good familiarity with the main ideas of the Christian faith, and appreciate their especial features. For many students and young people, this can be something of a problem. They may have only just begun the Christian life themselves, and still be on a steep learning curve! But rest assured that the time you invest in deepening your understanding of the Christian faith will be of benefit to you (as you appreciate more deeply the full richness of the gospel for yourself) and to your friends (as you realize the best ways of presenting the gospel with their situations in mind).

If you feel the need to do something about this, there is no reason why you should not join study groups meeting for this purpose, attend summer schools run by leading Christian institutions (most notably Regent College, Vancouver, with others in various regions of the Western world), or spend some time reading books written with these needs in mind (some suggestions are made at the end of this book).

In what follows, we shall provide outline sketches of some ways in which the full attraction of the Christian gospel can be explained, bearing in mind the human needs which we noted earlier. You can fill in the fine detail for yourself!

Hunger

Jesus is the 'bread of life' (John 6:48), who is able to satisfy the deepest human need. Anyone who eats anything else (even the manna given to Israel in the wilderness!) will end up hungering again. But Jesus Christ will provide a lasting solution to the human hunger for life in all its fullness. By feeding on him through coming to faith, we can begin something which nothing, not even death, can destroy (John 6:35–58).

Thirst

Like hunger, thirst is an indication of human emptiness and need. Jesus gives 'the water . . . [which] will become . . . a spring of water welling up to eternal life' (John 4:13–14). Anyone who drinks of any other water will thirst again; the water which Jesus gives, however, will not only quench the thirst of the present. It will become a resource which will remain present in the believer's life, and be a constant source of refreshment.

Emptiness

The French Christian writer Blaise Pascal once stated that there is a 'God-shaped gap' within each and every one of us. Everyone has a vacuum, a region of dissatisfaction, which we cannot help but notice. We may hope that this will be satisfied by a relationship, a career or by material wealth. Yet it doesn't work out. Why is it that there are so many unhappy rich people? For Pascal, as for Scripture, only God can fit the God-shaped gap within us. The deep and real sense of emptiness can only be ended by discovering something or someone who is able to correspond to the absence. As Scripture declares that our sadness and emptiness is due to the absence of God, the only genuine and lasting solution to our problem is to be found in God himself.

Loneliness

Many people have a deeply-rooted sense of loneliness, which may even occasionally take the form of despair. The gospel reminds us that we were created for fellowship with a loving, living, personal God, who demonstrates his love for us through the death of Jesus Christ. Loneliness is an inevitable result of being cut off from God through sin. By claiming the forgiveness which God graciously makes available through Christ, we may be reconciled to God (2 Corinthians 5:19), and know the peace and joy of being restored to fellowship with God. In addition, it means being adopted into the family of God, and being able to know a sense of security and belonging through being a member of his people.

Hopelessness

The future often seems bleak and hopeless. What is there to look forward to but death? Why bother living in the first place? These thoughts prey on the minds of a surprisingly large number of people. Yet discovering God provides both a reason to live and a reason to hope. To come to know God is like beginning a new relationship, which brings a new meaning and a new quality of life into being. Yet we are assured that this new life is not something we shall have to give up at death; it is *eternal life*, a life which we can begin to experience now, but which reaches its climax when we are finally united to Christ in the resurrection.

Lostness

The gospel declares that we are lost. We have wandered away from God through sin. However, in his great love and compassion, God has set out to find us and bring us home. We are like sheep who have gone astray. God is like the shepherd who sets out in search of the lost sheep, and will not rest until it has been found and safely brought home to the security of the sheepfold (Luke 15:3–7).

In each case, there is a considerable attraction to the gospel. It is up to you to work out how best to explain and develop these aspects of the gospel, and show your friends how the gospel scratches where they itch! One way of preparing for this is to give some thought to how you can speak briefly yet effectively about the nature and attraction of the gospel. We shall explore this in what follows.

Prepare a brief summary of the gospel message

Every now and then, you are going to be asked this question: 'What's Christianity all about, then?' And it is clear that you have about thirty seconds to answer! It helps to have a thumbnail sketch of the gospel at your fingertips, so that you can give a helpful reply even in such a brief time.

So how do you condense material, to make the best possible use of time? Here is a technique which I was taught many years ago by a colleague from the British Broadcasting Corporation. I will set out the basic method in what follows. You may find it helpful to do this with a friend, who will help you assess your performance and suggest improvements.

1. Allow yourself five minutes to say what you think needs to be said. Write down your reply to the question 'What's Christianity all about, then?' Take time to discover how much can be said in five minutes, and aim to make the best possible use of the time you have been allowed. When you are satisfied with your reply, read it out aloud, and establish how long it took you to say it. And don't cheat: you must speak at your normal rate!

2. Now ask yourself how effective your answer was. In particular, try to identify the core of your reply – the things that were absolutely essential, and that made your reply effective. Did you really need five minutes to say that? Or can you see ways of keeping that core, while reducing the time needed to say it? To find out, you must

condense that reply. In what follows, we shall look at some ways of developing the skill of condensation.

3. Now allow yourself just two minutes for your reply to the same question. Can you condense your reply into this much briefer period, while at the same time keeping its central message? Can you retain the content, while cutting down on the words needed? You will be surprised to discover how easy it is to get rid of redundant words.

4. Now allow yourself one minute . . .

5. . . . And now thirty seconds.

It will be obvious that you cannot say all that you would like to say in such a brief allocation of time. But by effective and thoughtful use of biblical material or your own experience, you can pave the way for a longer discussion later. Here are some suggestions for possible approaches.

Parables

Take a parable, such as the parable of the wasteful (or 'prodigal') son (Luke 15:11–32), which makes the point that a loving God is always waiting for his wayward children to come home. Can you see how this could be the basis of an effective summary of the gospel? See if you can write a thirty-second summary of the gospel on the basis of this parable. You could open your reply like this: 'Jesus told a parable which sums up the gospel very nicely. It's about . . .' There is no need to give the exact reference; just explain what it's all about.

Brief biblical passages

Try using brief biblical passages as summaries of the gospel. Especially suitable passages include the following: John 3:3 (which introduces the idea of being 'born again'); John 3:16 (which stresses the love of God); 1 Peter 1:3–4 (which brings out the hope of faith); John 6:51 (which points to the life-giving quality of the gospel); or Romans 5:6 (which identifies the sinfulness of humanity, and the remedy offered in the gospel). Remember that you cannot hope to say everything you would like to in so brief a space. Your reply could take the form: 'Jesus once described himself as the "bread of life". Well, I realized that I was hungry, looking for something which would give meaning and purpose to my life. And I found in Jesus someone who could satisfy that hunger, and give me new life. And I've never looked back.'

Paul's theological terms

In his letters, Paul uses a number of theological terms which can be invaluable summaries of the gospel. Terms such as 'salvation', 'adoption' and 'reconciliation' can allow you to explain the basic elements of the gospel. These terms will be explored later in this book. Your reply could take the following form: 'In one of his letters, Paul talks about "being reconciled to God in Christ". That's a great summary of what the gospel is all about. It's about being restored to a friendship with God who has been offended. It's about Jesus making possible a new relationship with God which makes life worth living. And that's just what I found . . .'

Personal experience

If you find it difficult to condense biblical material in the way suggested above, you can always talk about your own experience. Thirty seconds gives you enough time to tell your friends that Christianity is the best thing that ever happened to you – and why!

Notice that, if you are using biblical material, there is no need either to give an exact biblical reference for what you are saying ('Jesus once said . . .' is quite good enough for these introductory encounters). Nor is there even a need to produce a Bible. In fact, doing this might be counter-productive, given the very bad public image that 'Bible-bashers' have in student circles. Remember that this introductory conversation is just laying the foundation for a longer discussion later, when you will have ample time to study biblical passages together in private.

3

But I have this problem . . .

Some people feel very threatened by Christianity. They may find it convenient to seize upon certain points as obstacles to faith. In other words, they use some argument against Christianity as an excuse for not thinking further about the claims of Jesus Christ. 'Christianity is for the intellectually feeble.' 'I can't believe in God with all this suffering in the world.' 'Christianity is just for those who need a sense of purpose and meaning – and I don't!' 'Everybody knows that God is just an astronaut.' Sometimes, of course, these are genuine difficulties, and must be treated with respect. There are answers to these objections, and it is important that you should know them and be able to deploy them effectively.

Very often, however, these reasons are not genuine difficulties at all – they are simply ploys to prevent discussion of Christianity getting too intense or involved for comfort. Many non-Christians find a discussion of Christianity very threatening. They feel that they are being attacked, and they dig in to their positions. Just as someone who is drowning might clutch at a straw, so they reach for the nearest defence against Christianity they can find. Occasionally, these objections to Christianity have been picked up at second hand from books or magazine articles.

Why do many non-Christians find Christianity so threatening? Because Christianity involves a demand. It involves a demand for conversion, for a change of life. It involves repentance – an admission that you are wrong, that you are sinful. And these are difficult things for many people to accept. They feel that by admitting them, they will be losing face. When you talk to your non-Christian friends about your faith, your friends may feel that you are passing judgment on them (for example, by describing them as sinners), and become very uncomfortable. Their natural response may well be to mount a counter-attack by raising an objection to Christian belief – not necessarily because this is a genuine difficulty for them, but because it sidetracks the conversation in a less threatening direction.

Let's look at an example to bring out this point. Imagine that Julia, who is a Christian, is talking to her non-Christian friend Michelle, and the conversation has got round to Christianity.

Julia Christianity is about the love of God for us. I wonder if you can see just how much God loves you, Michelle?

Michelle (looking very uncomfortable, starts to say something, then changes her mind) Er . . .

Julia Just think, Michelle, Jesus Christ died for you? Isn't that amazing. He died for you!

Michelle But I can't see how you can talk about God being loving when there's all this suffering in the world. How can you reconcile that with God being love?

Julia Well, Michelle, that's a fair question. Let me tell you what the famous Oxford philosopher of religion Richard Swinburne has to say about the problem of evil . . .

Can you see what's going on in this conversation? Michelle feels that she is being threatened by Julia. Julia's statements are not about Christianity in general, but are directed at Michelle in particular. Michelle handles this situation by sidetracking Julia into a general discussion about the problem of suffering. Now Julia has to deal with *this*, when she would much rather be talking about the love of God for Michelle! Now it may be that Michelle has genuine difficulties with this problem. However, the main function of this tactic is to remove the personal threat which Michelle felt on account of the way the discussion was going! The discussion is no longer about God and Michelle, but about how philosophers handle the problem of suffering!

Think about people as well as issues!

When you're discussing Christianity with your friends, you must realize that the claims of Jesus Christ are one element – by far the most important element, to be sure – in your discussion. The other element is the person you're talking to. And it is the second element which it is all too easy to neglect.

You must appreciate that you are not arguing with a computer, or some sort of machine, but with fellow human beings. They will have emotions, feelings, and possibly deeply-held views. You must be sensitive to their interests and feelings and avoid making it unnecessarily difficult for them to come to faith. Remember that your friends may well identify *you* with the Christian faith – and that means that you may put obstacles in their path to faith because of the way you relate to them. To become a Christian is a difficult enough decision – don't make it even more difficult for them because of the way you handle them. Try to make it as easy as possible for them to turn to Jesus Christ and his gospel.

A failure to deal sensitively with someone can be disastrous. You need to be aware of certain basic human emotions and feelings, such as the need to feel that you have been listened to. Try to be a good listener. It may be that your friends have had experiences which have made it genuinely difficult for them to take Christianity seriously. It may be that they have a genuine difficulty which you can help resolve. Let them know that you are listening to them, and trying to understand them. Understanding people doesn't mean that you have to agree with them! If it is obvious that you are taking trouble to listen to them, they will find it much easier to listen to you.

Try to imagine what happens when some people sharing in a discussion feel threatened by the way things are going, and so 'dig in' to their position in such a way that they can't move without losing face. They will dig themselves in by erecting defensive barricades that you can't penetrate. No amount of arguing will get you anywhere here. They don't want to give the impression of backing down. They may well sense that you are right – but they feel that they will seem to lose face with you or with their circle of friends if they admit this. So how do you avoid this situation?

You need to appreciate that people tend to see their ideas as part of their person. This means that if you attack their ideas, you may give the impression that you are attacking them as people. An attack on your friends' views on a matter such as the resurrection may thus be seen as an attack on your friends themselves, even though this isn't what you were intending. You must therefore be careful to distinguish the two. Let's look at two different ways of handling your friends' difficulties with the resurrection. Let's suppose they have just finished listing their difficulties with the idea. Here are two different responses. Try to image the effect they would have on their intended audiences.

A. Well, I'm sorry, but you're wrong. These objections just aren't important. I can't take them seriously, and I don't think you've even bothered to think about them. I'm sure that if you were to think about them longer, you'd see that. Let's go through these so-called objections that you've just made, and I'll show you how unimportant they really are.

B. I can understand just how you must feel about this. In fact, I once felt much the same way myself, and can really sympathize with you. Actually, I've changed my mind since then, and see it in a different way now. Let me try and explain the way I see it.

Approach A tends to identify people and their views, and suggests that you're trying to score points off them by beating them in argument. It's you and your ideas against them and their ideas. Approach B makes it easy for your friends to make a distinction between themselves as persons and their ideas on the resurrection. You are avoiding attacking your friends unnecessarily. It suggests that you are trying to help them think the matter through (which is what you are, or ought, to be doing). You are seen as giving another perspective on the question, rather than as contradicting your friends. In short, you are making it much easier for your friends to listen to you. It isn't you against them as opponents, but you and them together trying to resolve something in which you're mutually interested. Nobody is going to lose face in this discussion. Your friendship will survive B, and probably benefit from it – but **A** may well wreck it! A 'lock-in' situation is very likely to result if you fail to separate the people and the issue, and cause them to lose face with their friends.

So if some of your friends inform you that they have given full consideration to the claims of Christianity, and have decided to reject it – don't necessarily feel obliged to take this at face value. They may just be stalling (in other words, they haven't bothered to think about Christianity at all, and don't intend to if they can avoid it!). Or they may have encountered a watered-down version of Christianity, and rightly dismissed it as boring and irrelevant. Perhaps you can help them realize that this is just a caricature of Christianity by presenting them with the real thing. Or they may have genuine difficulties with some particular point, and these difficulties act as obstacles in their path to faith. Perhaps you are the one who could remove these obstacles – or at least show them up in a different light. But you must be sensitive to their feelings in doing so!

Removing obstacles to faith

You cannot argue people into the kingdom of God! It may be that you are able to win an argument with your non-Christian friends. For example, you may end up convincing them that God does indeed exist. Yet that still leaves them a long way from faith. In the end, Christian faith comes about by meeting the risen Christ, not just by becoming convinced of the truth of some arguments! Christianity isn't just a list of propositions which you can tick off as you accept them. It is a matter of the heart, as well as the mind. And there's always the danger that you may win the argument, but lose your friend. Why bother, then, dealing with difficulties which people might have about Christianity? Because these difficulties are obstacles between them and God, which we are in a position to remove or at least to weaken. Your arguments won't bring them to faith – but they may remove obstacles in the path of that faith.

Think of each person as having a personal road to faith. In some cases, this will be short and simple, with few obstacles along the way. For others, it may be long and complex, with many barriers to be overcome. The problem is that we don't know what sort of road we are dealing with! We have no idea of how long it may take someone to come to faith, or what the problems may be.

Some find this very discouraging. Yet there is no reason why this should happen. The important thing is this: every step they take along the way is a step nearer to faith. You may not be able to bring them all the way to a final commitment to Jesus Christ – but you can leave them closer to that goal than when they started. So don't get discouraged if you don't bring all your friends to faith! Your task is to bring them closer to faith, even if you don't have the privilege of bringing them all the way. I have met many people who have told me that what first got them thinking about Christianity was something that someone said to them many years ago. Yet that person has since died, without knowing that what they said was instrumental in setting someone on the road which finally led to coming to faith. So never be discouraged if your efforts seem unrewarded! You are planting seeds, which will grow in God's own good time.

In the final analysis, of course, there is only one agent in evangelism, and that is God himself. It is his gospel and his power, wisdom and strength lie behind it. Our task as believers is to point people in the right direction, so that they may encounter the living God. In John's gospel we find a very helpful pointer to the nature of evangelism (John 1:43-51). Philip tells Nathanael that he has found the person about whom Moses and all the prophets wrote – Jesus of Nazareth. Nathanael immediately raises objections to this. How can such a person come from Nazareth, of all places?

Philip might have begun a long argument about how this objection wasn't as serious as might at first seem. He might have appealed to the same prophecy that we find cited in Matthew's gospel (Matthew 2:23). Rather than get involved in a rather contentious argument about Old Testament prophecy and the merits of Nazareth as a town, Philip issues a simple and direct invitation: 'Come and see' (John 1:46). And, as the remainder of the passage makes clear, it is Jesus who captures Nathanael's heart and mind (John 1:47-51).

Or again, think of John the Baptist (Mark 1:1-9; John 1:15-36). He pointed people away from himself, to the one who was greater than himself. He was like a herald, a royal forerunner, proclaiming the coming of the king. Like him, we point away from ourselves, away from our own faith – and we point to Jesus Christ, the one who is greater than us, upon whom our faith is based.

It is our job to be a signpost – like Philip and John the Baptist. We too have to point people away from ourselves and towards the living Christ. It isn't our arguments which may bring someone to faith – it is a personal encounter with the risen Christ. We may help create conditions favourable to that encounter. Our task is to remove impediments to this encounter.

What sort of impediments? The following are common obstacles placed between individuals and the God who loved them so much that he gave his only Son to die for them (John 3:16):

1. misunderstandings of what Christianity is all about;
2. genuine intellectual obstacles, such as doubts about the fundamental goodness or love of God;

3. ignorance about what to do in order to become a Christian;

4. a reluctance to admit to being a sinner.

This is not to say that we can remove all the obstacles to faith for our friends! For, in the end, the greatest obstacle which comes between an individual and God is that individual's sin. Only that individual can deal with this sin, by recognizing and admitting it and receiving forgiveness from God. What we can do is to show our friends that it is sin which is the real obstacle between them and the living God. By removing, or helping to reduce, other difficulties in the path of faith, we can explain what the real difficulty is, and how it may be resolved. This is the task of evangelism – to identify the real problem (human sin), and proclaim (and explain!) the one genuine solution (divine forgiveness).

In these first few chapters, we've been looking at some points worth noting as you try to explain Christianity to your friends. They may help you avoid some obvious mistakes. But, as we noted right at the beginning, there is no substitute for thinking through the main points of the Christian faith yourself. You can get away with 'Actually, I don't know!' or 'I haven't thought about that one!' every now and then – but when it becomes a regular occurrence, you aren't likely to be terribly helpful to anyone interested in learning more about Christianity. The remainder of this little book is an attempt to help you think about the main points of the Christian faith, so that you can explain it and defend it to your interested friends. We begin by going right to the core of the Christian faith, as we begin to think about Jesus Christ himself.

Part 2

Questions about . . .

4

Jesus

Since the coming of Jesus, history has never been the same. Two great epochs – before Christ and after Christ – are defined. It's one of the little ironies of history that we date everyone and everything (including those who did their best to exterminate Christianity!) with reference to this one man. For the Roman historian Livy, everything was to be dated with reference to the founding of Rome. But for Western culture, everything is to be dated with reference to the birth of Jesus Christ. Even the lives of those who were utterly opposed to Jesus Christ and all that he stood for are dated with reference to him! Thus the Roman emperor Nero died in AD 68, and the great dictator Joseph Stalin in AD 1953.

So what relevance does Jesus have for us? Why is it that Christianity centres upon this man? Even at this stage, a number of serious misunderstandings can arise as non-Christians attempt to make sense of Jesus' relevance for the Christian. For example, a Marxist might assume that Jesus has the same relevance for Christianity that Karl Marx has for Marxism – someone who introduced some new ideas into history. And even some less-informed Christians seem to think that this is why Jesus is so important for Christianity. In this chapter, we're going to look at a number of important misunderstandings and objections which you are likely to come across as you try to explain Christianity to your friends.

One important point needs to be made before we do this. Some Christians tend to assume that people are either totally for Christ, or totally opposed to him. In fact, the situation is much more complex. Many people feel sympathetic to Jesus, yet wouldn't regard themselves as Christians. They may, for example, be prepared to accept Jesus as a great teacher, or perhaps as a prophet – but not to accept him as Saviour and Lord. Now this step may take place very suddenly – but it may also take place in a number of stages. For example, someone might begin by believing that Jesus didn't really exist. Then they might abandon this position, and start to think of Jesus as a good religious teacher. And finally, they might come to believe in him as Lord and Saviour.

So be sensitive: try to work out how far your friends have got in their thinking, and see if you can help them further along. And don't get discouraged if you find you only make slow progress – you may be helping your friends take a further step along the road which leads to faith. Now it may well be the case that you can help them come fully to faith. But don't necessarily become anxious if you are unable to help them believe in Jesus as Lord and Saviour straight away! Perhaps your friend may begin by believing that Jesus didn't actually exist, and ends up thinking of Jesus as a prophet. Later you, or perhaps someone else, can help him or her take the final steps. The important thing is to leave someone further along the road to faith in Christ than they were to begin with.

Jesus didn't exist anyway

This is an objection which isn't taken terribly seriously by anyone, but which you may still come across occasionally. The New Testament witness to Jesus is just too consistent and coherent to make this suggestion plausible. To account for it in other ways involves bringing in a whole series of rather improbable hypotheses. In the end, the simplest, neatest and most plausible explanation of the evidence is that Jesus of Nazareth existed as a historical person.

Perhaps, however, someone might point out that Paul hardly ever makes reference to the earthly life of Jesus. This is true in one respect. Paul is intensely interested in Jesus' death on the cross and his resurrection, but seems to make little reference to the details of Jesus' earthly life. But why should he anyway? Paul encountered the risen Christ – as have so many since him – and insists that it is this risen Christ, rather than the historical figure of Jesus of Nazareth, which is central to Christianity. We can hardly draw the conclusion that Jesus didn't exist on the basis of this evidence!

A further point concerns the nature of Paul's writings. The writings of Paul preserved in the New Testament are *letters*. They aren't history textbooks! It isn't relevant to Paul's purpose to go over the details of Jesus' life – he assumes that his readers already know these. Yet Paul often recalls the teaching of Jesus. This is especially clear in 1 Corinthians, in which Paul frequently calls upon the authority of Jesus to make a point (1 Corinthians 7:10; 9:14; 11:23–25). Paul argues that his teaching here goes back to the words of Jesus himself.

Paul's teaching at other points also seems to go back to Jesus, with strong traces of the precise words of Jesus being evident at a number of critical points in Paul's writings. It is clear that Paul's emphasis falls upon the relevance of the risen Christ to the Christian church – but that he draws upon the teaching authority of the earthly Jesus at points. Once more, there is no reason whatsoever to draw the extravagant conclusion that Jesus didn't exist.

It's like the suggestion that it was really Judas who died on the cross, or that Jesus wandered off to India after the disciples thought he had died: they are all suggestions which are totally unwarranted by the historical evidence.

The New Testament is biased

It might be argued, however, that the New Testament is biased. After all, it was written by Christians. We need independent confirmation of what the New Testament says about Jesus. We need to look at other sources.

But what sources are there? Our main sources for a knowledge of any aspect of the first century are Roman historians. These historians are few in number in the first place, and their writings largely exist as fragments. And they could hardly have foreseen that what seemed in the first century to be nothing more than an obscure Palestinian sect would one day come to dominate the Roman empire! Judea was a backwater of the Roman empire, to which nobody paid much attention in the first place. And anyway, thousands of Jewish agitators were crucified in Judea under the Romans: one more would have passed unnoticed.

In fact, we find exactly what we might expect: Roman historians pay no attention to Christianity at all, except when it causes social or political disturbances. Even then, their chief interest concerns these disturbances, rather than the basis of the beliefs of those who were causing them.

In the modern period, of course, news gathering has become much more sophisticated. News analysts can be jetted to any part of the world immediately to report on events which seem important. Their back-up teams can then provide in-depth analysis. But in the first century, Roman historians were based at Rome, and had to use material readily available to them. There was just no way that they could have known that seemingly unimportant events in an obscure provincial backwater would one day shake the empire to its foundations!

Having said that, we find reference to Jesus in four classical authors of the first or early second centuries. These are Thallus (a first-century Greek writer with a particular interest in relating Roman history to the history of the eastern Mediterranean, referred to by Julius Africanus in the third century); Pliny the Younger, writing around AD 111 to Trajan about the rapid spread of Christianity in Asia Minor; Tacitus, who wrote in approximately AD 115 concerning the events of AD 64, in which Nero made Christians the scapegoats for the burning of Rome; and Suetonius, writing around AD 120 concerning certain events in the reign of the emperor Claudius. Suetonius refers to a certain 'Chrestus' who was behind rioting at Rome. 'Christus' was still an unfamiliar name to Romans at this stage, whereas 'Chrestus' was a common name for slaves (meaning 'someone who is useful'). Even in the third and fourth centuries, Christian writers were still complaining about people who mis-spelled 'Christus' as 'Chrestus'!

What do these pagan authors tell us about Jesus? Not as much as we would like! Nevertheless, it is obvious that we can draw the following conclusions from their writings.

1. Christ had been condemned to death by Pontius Pilate, procurator of Judea, during the reign of the Roman emperor Tiberius (Tacitus). Pilate was procurator of Judea from AD 26–36, while Tiberius reigned from AD 14–37. The traditional date for the crucifixion is some point around AD 30–33.

2. At the time of the crucifixion, there was some sort of supernatural darkness, which some explained in terms of a total eclipse of the sun (Thallus).

3. By the time of Nero, Christ had attracted sufficient

followers in Rome to make them a suitable scapegoat for the burning of Rome. These followers were named 'Christians' after him (Tacitus).

4. 'Chrestus' was the founder of a distinctive sect within Judaism (Suetonius).

5. In AD 111, Christians worshipped Jesus as if he were God, abandoning the worship of the Roman emperor to do so (Pliny).

These historical details tie in well with the New Testament accounts. Fragmentary though they are, they are remarkably consistent with the New Testament witness.

What, then, about the allegation that the New Testament is biased? In one sense, it is obvious that this point is valid. The New Testament writers are out to win faith. They believe that their accounts of Jesus' life, death and resurrection ought to evoke faith in their readers (John 20:31). But in another sense, the point is not valid: the assumption of many critics of Christianity seems to be that the New Testament is inaccurate, perhaps deliberately distorting history for its own ends. New Testament scholarship has, however, actually tended to emphasize the historical reliability of the New Testament. The New Testament writers are indeed out to win faith – but it is clear that they believe that they can do this simply by recounting, rather than distorting or inventing, the history of Jesus Christ.

But the gospel accounts date from decades after the events they describe

There may be as many as thirty years separating the crucifixion of Jesus and the writing down of Mark's gospel. But so what? The implication seems to be that the gospel accounts are inaccurate, or unreliable, because of this gap. But by the standards of the time, this is actually a very short gap. To make this point, let's look at the biographies we possess of someone else living at more or less the same time – the emperor Tiberius, who reigned from AD 14–37.

Curiously, just as we depend primarily upon four gospels for our knowledge of the earthly life of Jesus, we are dependent primarily upon four biographies for our knowledge of Tiberius. One of these is clearly the work of an amateur, and is generally regarded as totally unreliable – and that is the earliest biography. The three most reliable biographies are those of Tacitus (dating from around AD 115), Suetonius (dating from about AD 120) and Dio Cassius (written approximately AD 230). Yet these were written between eighty and two hundred years after the death of their subject! The time-lapse in the case of the gospels is small in comparison.

Anyway, we mustn't think that the gospel writers had to sit down decades afterwards and try to remember what Jesus said and did! Modern New Testament studies have emphasized that the period between Jesus' death and the writing down of the first gospel saw what Jesus said and did being passed down faithfully by word of mouth. Nowadays, of course, we are used to recording words in writing or on magnetic tape. We seem to have lost the ability to remember long stories. Yet, in the ancient world, long stories – like Homer's *Iliad* and *Odyssey* – were remembered and retold. If you read one of these nowadays, you would react with amazement if it was suggested that you memorize it and repeat it to someone else! They're just so long! It was, however, done regularly in the ancient world.

What we find in the gospels, then, are accounts of what Jesus said and did, passed down faithfully by word of mouth for about three decades, and then written down. As New Testament studies emphasize, we possess a remarkably reliable account of what Jesus said and did.

Indeed, it is potentially better than anything we have about the emperor Tiberius!

Isn't Jesus just a good religious teacher?

Many critics of Christianity suggest that Jesus is simply a good religious teacher, like Socrates. Why, they ask, should they treat Jesus as being any different? Why should they listen to him, rather than any of the countless religious teachers in history? A number of points can be made in response to this important objection.

Christians don't think of Jesus as a dead rabbi

Of course Jesus is a religious teacher. Nobody denies that. The question is whether he was just a religious teacher, or whether he was far more than that.

It is virtually impossible to read the gospel accounts of Jesus' ministry without being impressed by what he says. He taught with authority (Mark 1:27). But Christians have always regarded Jesus as being far more than a Jewish religious teacher, or rabbi. This is obvious from the way they talk about him. They talk about 'being saved by Jesus', and refer to Jesus as 'Lord,' 'Saviour' and 'Redeemer'. They may even refer to him as 'God incarnate'. The gospels themselves certainly present us with Jesus' teaching – but they focus far more than might be expected upon his death and what happened afterwards. Indeed, one respected New Testament scholar has suggested that Mark's gospel is basically an account of Jesus' death with an extended introduction!

We need more than just religious teaching if we're going to be saved

In his book *Mere Christianity*, C. S. Lewis makes a vitally important point concerning the identity of Jesus:

We never have followed the advice of great teachers. Why are we likely to begin now? Why are we more likely to follow Christ than any of the others? Because he's the best moral teacher? But that makes it even less likely that we shall follow him. If we can't take the elementary lessons, is it likely that we're going to take the more advanced one? If Christianity only means one more bit of good advice, then Christianity is of no importance. There's been no lack of good advice over the last four thousand years. A bit more makes no difference.

The point Lewis is making is that we need more than someone who can just give us advice – we need someone who can change our situation.

St Paul makes much the same point at Romans 7:17–25. There seems to be something about human nature which makes it want to do good, but prevents it from doing so. Something prevents us from doing the good things we'd like to. More than this, something seems to influence us to do things which we know are wrong. Paul identifies this 'something' as sin, which he understands as a force working within us.

Yet it is not just Christians who recognize that there is something wrong with human nature. Many of the more serious attempts by atheists to understand the mystery of human nature end up speaking about 'a fatal flaw' in our nature. Just telling us what is right and what is wrong doesn't help us, if there is something about us that prevents us from doing right and avoiding wrong! Yet Paul declares that Jesus Christ does far more than just teach us – he delivers us from the power of sin (Romans 7:24–25). He breaks the stranglehold of sin, and sets us free.

Let's take this point a little further. What's the point in telling people not to be frightened about death, if death really does mark the grim end of everything? But if someone could change that situation, could show us that death wasn't the end, or could assure us that anyone who believed in him would be raised from the dead – well, that would be something rather different, wouldn't it? Already we can see the importance of the resurrection in connection with the relevance of Jesus!

The resurrection points to Jesus being far more than just a good teacher

There has been no shortage of human religious teachers. The problem is deciding which ones to take seriously, and which to dismiss as cranks. At the time of the French Revolution, a whole series of new religions came into being, each with its own special teacher. Many thought that Christianity was a thing of the past, and so invented new religions to take its place. Yet none of them seemed to be able to capture the imagination of the general public. They attracted no followers, and most ended up collapsing after a few months or years. In desperation, one of the inventors of these new religions approached the great French statesman, Talleyrand. He asked how his religion could get off the ground. 'My dear fellow,' Talleyrand is supposed to have replied, 'I suggest that you get yourself crucified and then rise again on the third day.'

Only Jesus has ever been raised from the dead. The New Testament, of course, tells us about individuals (such as Lazarus: John 11:1–44) who were brought back from the dead by Jesus. Nevertheless, these individuals were brought back from the dead, only to die again. In the case of Jesus, we are dealing with someone who was raised from the dead, never to die again. Death's hold on him was completely broken. And the New Testament also emphasizes that Jesus was raised from the dead by God himself. Lazarus and Jairus' daughter may have been raised by Jesus – but Jesus himself was raised from the dead by God.

Of course, your friends may not believe that Jesus rose from the dead – and in the next chapter, we'll look at some of their difficulties. But the resurrection, if it really happened, immediately sets Jesus in a class of his own. He is unique. He is indeed a religious teacher – but he is far more than this. It is not wrong to say that Jesus was a great religious teacher: it is just inadequate. It doesn't go far enough. There is so much more that needs to be said! He is the risen Lord, who is able to encounter us, just as he encountered Paul on that road to Damascus. Here is no dead rabbi from the past, who now rots in some forgotten Palestinian grave – here is the living and risen Lord.

Why do Christians believe in the divinity of Jesus?

Few people have any difficulty in accepting that Jesus was a man. The difficulties start with the belief that he is also God. The divinity of Christ is frequently challenged by critics of Christianity, who often suggest that the first Christians rushed uncritically to the conclusion that Jesus was God. The evidence, however, points in a rather different direction, showing that the first Christians were actually extremely reluctant to conclude that Jesus was God. After all, every Jew knew that there was only one God – suggesting that Jesus was God would have been a very difficult conclusion to draw. The only reason it *was* drawn was that the evidence in its favour was so overwhelming. For example, Thomas' famous declaration – 'My Lord and my God!' (John 20:28) – was made only after he was absolutely convinced that Jesus really had risen from the dead. Let's look at the reasons underlying the characteristic Christian belief that Jesus is divine.

The New Testament often describes Jesus as doing things which only God can do

The Old Testament emphasized that God alone can save (see Isaiah 45:21–22). There was no saviour apart from God himself. Yet the New Testament talks about Jesus being our saviour (Acts 4:12; Hebrews 2:10). Jesus is the 'Saviour' and 'Christ the Lord' (Luke 2:11). Titus 2:13–14 refers to 'our great God and Saviour, Jesus Christ, who gave himself for us to redeem us from all wickedness'. An especially interesting passage is Titus 1:3–4: verse 3 refers to God as 'our Saviour', and verse 4 to Jesus Christ as 'our Saviour'. The implications of this passage are obvious and profound. A fish came to be a symbol of faith for the early Christians, because the five letters of the Greek word for 'fish' (*ichthus*) was an acronym for 'Jesus Christ, Son of God, Saviour.' Here Jesus is clearly understood to do something which only God can do – saving us.

Similarly, only God can forgive sins. Yet Jesus forgave sins. Mark 2:1–7 shows the outrage felt by the Jews when Jesus forgave the sins of a paralysed man. 'Son, your sins are forgiven' – and immediately, the Jews rightly asked, 'Who can forgive sins but God alone?' They were absolutely right. None but God can forgive sins – yet Jesus did forgive sins. What are we to make of this? C. S. Lewis made this point forcefully in *Mere Christianity*:

> Unless the speaker is God, this is really so preposterous as to be comic. We can all understand how a man forgives offences against himself. You tread on my toe and I forgive you, you steal my money and I forgive you. But what should we make of a man, himself unrobbed and untrodden on, who announced that he forgave you for treading on other men's toes and stealing other men's money. Asinine fatuity is the kindest

description we should give of his conduct. Yet this is what Jesus did. He told people that their sins were forgiven, and never waited to consult all the other people whom their sins had undoubtedly injured. He unhesitatingly behaved as if he was the party chiefly concerned, the person chiefly offended in all offences. This makes sense only if he really was the God whose laws are broken and whose love is wounded in every sin. In the mouth of any speaker who is not God, these words would imply what I can only regard as a silliness and conceit unrivalled by any other character in history . . . I am trying here to prevent anyone saying the really foolish thing that people often say about him: 'I'm ready to accept Jesus as a great moral teacher, but I don't accept his claim to be God.' This is the one thing we must not say. A man who was merely a man and said the sort of things Jesus said would not be a great moral teacher.

By claiming to forgive sins, Jesus claims to be able to do something which only God can do.

The New Testament refers to Jesus in terms which imply that he is God

Three particularly important New Testament passages should be noted: John 1:1–18; Hebrews 2:9–18; and Philippians 2:5–11. You will find it helpful to read these along with a good commentary, which brings out the importance of each of the passages for our understanding of the full relevance of Jesus. Jesus is 'the word become flesh'. He is one who humbled himself, taking upon himself human nature with all its weaknesses in order to redeem us. He is Emmanuel, 'God with us'.

There are also many other very important passages, of which we can only note a few. For example, compare Joel 2:32 with Acts 2:21. In his prophecy, Joel refers to some period in the future, when the Spirit of God will be poured out on everyone, and when 'everyone who calls on the name of the Lord will be saved'. Now the 'Lord' in question is the Lord God himself. But Acts 2:21 understands this to be a reference to Jesus, who God has made 'both Lord and Christ' (Acts 2:36) through his resurrection from the dead (and notice the importance of the resurrection in this connection). In other words, a biblical passage which refers to God is understood by the New Testament to refer to Jesus, on account of the resurrection. Exactly the same thing can be seen happening in Philippians 2:10–11. Here Paul refers to every knee bowing to the name of Jesus Christ – but he is referring to an Old Testament prophecy (Isaiah 45:23) which speaks of every knee bowing to God. There are, of course, other passages which clearly imply the divinity of Jesus – for example, John 20:28, in which Thomas addresses Jesus as 'My Lord and my God'. Hebrews 1:8 equates Jesus with God by quoting a psalm addressed to the Lord God, and referring it to the Lord Jesus.

Many other New Testament passages which do not explicitly state that Jesus is divine certainly tend to point in that direction. It is obvious that the New Testament regards Jesus as an agent or representative of God, who had a unique relationship with God. He showed us what God is like, and was able to speak with divine authority (John 14:8–14). When Jesus promised eternal life to all who believe in him, we know that God stands behind this promise, which is made on God's behalf, and with God's authority. Jesus is understood to act as God and for God.

All these considerations clearly point to the conclusion that Jesus is God. We are not dealing with just one isolated piece of evidence pointing to this conclusion, but with the cumulative force of many pieces of evidence, all of which converge. The resurrection; what Jesus said; what Jesus did; what the first Christians believed about him – all these pieces of evidence, and others besides, have their part to play in building up to the crucial conclusion that Jesus is divine. It is a crucial conclusion, and the books suggested for further reading will help you justify and explain it to your friends. We now move on to consider the importance of this conclusion.

Jesus was male, so has no relevance to women

Some critics of Christianity object to it on the basis of the maleness of Jesus Christ. Any religion with a male saviour, they argue, degrades women. This is not true, it must be emphasized. But it is important to understand why it is not true. There would be substance to the objection only if it could be shown that Christians used the maleness of Jesus as an excuse for declaring the superiority of males over females. Paul, however, makes it clear that all are equal in Christ. 'There is neither Jew nor Greek, slave nor free, male nor female, for you are all one in Christ Jesus' (Galatians 3:28).

So how important is it that Jesus was a man? The fact that he was a real human being, in addition to being divine, is of vital importance to Christianity. If Jesus was not truly human, he would have no point of contact with us. He would be a stranger to the human situation. We would not be able to relate to him. There is, however, a deeper issue here. How important is it that Jesus was *male*? Many women wonder if they are somehow disadvantaged by the fact that God chose to become incarnate as a male, rather than a female.

The gospel centres on a series of central affirmations. Whoever believes in Jesus Christ will have eternal life.

Whoever calls upon the name of the Lord will be saved. Whoever repents of their sins will be forgiven. These promises are made to all, irrespective of gender or nationality. And they are grounded in what God achieved in and through Jesus Christ. The doctrine of the incarnation affirms that God enters into our human situation, sharing its sorrows and griefs, in order to transform that situation. God chose to become human, in order that we might be reconciled to him. To put it crudely, this entailed either becoming a male or a female. Yet the *particularity* of the gender of the redeemer does not in any way imply a corresponding limitation on the scope of redemption. Christ was a Jew; he died to redeem both Jews and Gentiles. Christ was a male; he died to redeem both males and females. Jesus was an Aramaic-speaker who brings salvation to those who spoke or speak Aramaic, Latin, English or Cantonese. His nationality, gender, blood group and hair colour have no bearing upon the scope of redemption. Equally, chronology has no bearing upon the scope of redemption. It is not simply those who were alive at the same time as Jesus who can be redeemed by him; the saving power of the risen Christ is both prospective and retrospective.

By choosing to enter into history as one of us, it was inevitable that God would commit himself to a set of specific historical circumstances in the incarnation. The incarnate God would possess a specific nationality, culture, gender, language, blood group, and hair colour. But the *particularities* of the incarnation must be set against the *universality* of the redemption which is thereby made possible. The central affirmation of the incarnation is that God became one of us, in order to redeem us – not that he became a first-century male Palestinian Jew. No culture, gender, or language is given enhanced priority on account of the incarnation, nor can people of any culture, gender or language be regarded as 'second-class' Christians.

The idea that Jesus is divine is unnecessary

For some critics of Christianity, the divinity of Christ is quite unnecessary. If we didn't accept his divinity, a much simpler version of Christianity would result. It would be much simpler to understand and believe. Why bother believing in the divinity of Christ? As we saw in the last section, one important reason is that it is right! It may be difficult – but if it is right, we have little choice but to accept it. Yet some critics of Christianity seem to think that you can get rid of the idea of the divinity of Christ, and leave every other Christian doctrine untouched. They seem to think it's like some sort of precision surgery, allowing you to remove apparently unnecessary parts of the human body (like the appendix), leaving everything else untouched. But in fact, removing the divinity of Christ from Christianity is like removing the heart from the human body – it's not taking away something unimportant, but the very source of its life and power! These words of C. S. Lewis sum up the situation perfectly: 'The doctrine of Christ's divinity seems to me not something stuck on which you can unstick, but something that peeps out at every point so that you'd have to unravel the whole web to get rid of it.' To deny the divinity of Christ is *unnecessary* and leads to a totally *inadequate* version of Christianity. Let's see what happens if we abandon belief in the divinity of Christ.

Suffering becomes an even greater problem

One of the difficulties for Christianity felt by many people is caused by suffering. God seems to stand aloof from the suffering of the world. It seems that God does not know what suffering involves. He seems to be distant from his world, uninvolved in its suffering. We suffer, while God does not. But for Christianity, Jesus is the suffering God incarnate. He knows and understands what it is like to suffer. God isn't like some general sitting in his bomb-proof bunker miles from the front line. He is one who has already fought in the same fight as his followers. God already knows what it is like to live upon earth as a man. He knows, and understands, what it means to be human. The whole problem of suffering takes on a new meaning, when we realize that God suffered in Jesus Christ.

We need more than a good religious teacher

Throughout our long history, we have had lots of religious teachers. What good is one more? If Jesus is simply a man, he shares the common human problem – sin, suffering and death. If Jesus is just a human being, like us, then he is not the solution to the human problem. What we need is someone who will change the human situation, not just tell us more about it. The Christian assertion that Jesus is God incarnate tells us that God has come into the world and become involved with it. It changes our understanding of what God is like. It forces us to give up silly or inadequate views of God – like God being totally distant and remote, and unconcerned for his world. It forces us to give up inadequate views of Jesus – like Jesus being just a good religious teacher.

It tells us that Jesus is someone unique. He, and he alone among people, is God. It sets him apart from all other religious teachers. It gives weight to his teaching and actions. If Jesus is not divine, he's not the solution to the human situation – he's part of the problem. After all, religious teachers are just other human beings like us. They may be superior morally and intellectually but they are still merely humans. They can't change the human situation. They view the human situation from the same standpoint as ourselves. They're in the same boat as the rest of us – and the boat seems to be sinking fast.

But what if someone comes from outside the human situation? What happens if someone comes who sees us through the eyes of God? What if someone breaks down the wall of death? What if someone draws its sting? What if we are redeemed through the death of the Son of God on the cross? The insight that Jesus is God himself, that he is God incarnate, immediately identifies Jesus as being of enormous significance – because God himself has intervened in our situation in order to transform it. Jesus isn't part of the human problem – he holds the key to its solution. Yet that insight is only upheld adequately by belief in his divinity – a belief, which, as we have seen, is thoroughly grounded in the biblical evidence.

The cross no longer shows the love of God
Christianity has always insisted that the death of Jesus Christ on the cross shows the love of God for us. It is a very tender insight, one which is central to the Christian faith. Many people who have difficulty with the idea of the divinity of Christ have no difficulty with the idea of God's love being demonstrated in the death of Jesus Christ at Calvary. In fact, however, this invaluable insight depends in the first place upon Jesus' divinity. If Jesus isn't God, then his death shows nothing more than the love of one man for his friends. It is a demonstration of human, not divine, love. History is littered with people who have given their lives for their friends. What is so special about Jesus doing the same?

The only adequate answer is that Jesus was different. He wasn't an ordinary human being. This was no merely human act of love, but the love of God in action. In the tragic scene of Jesus Christ trudging towards his place of execution, we see none other than God himself, showing the full extent of his love for us to the world. As Charles Wesley puts it in his great hymn *And can it be?*:

Amazing love! how can it be
That thou, my God, shouldst die for me?

To abandon faith in Christ's divinity is to lose the insight that the death of Jesus Christ shows forth the love of God for us. This just goes to prove the point C. S. Lewis made earlier – that the divinity of Christ underlies far more of the Christian faith than many people realize. It cannot be removed without destroying the Christian faith. And as we have seen, there is no case whatsoever for its elimination.

It will be obvious that one major topic which has already been mentioned in this chapter is the resurrection itself. Yet many people have difficulty with the idea of the resurrection of Jesus. In view of its importance, we will discuss some of these difficulties in the next chapter.

5

The resurrection

The New Testament is dominated by the resurrection of Jesus. 'He is risen!' is the theme which sounds again and again in its pages. It is the risen Lord who commissions his disciples, and sends them out to win all nations (Matthew 28:17–20). It was the risen Lord who encountered Saul on the road to Damascus. It is the same risen Lord whom we know and experience. 'But,' a critic might say, 'I am not really sure that the resurrection happened in the first place. In fact, I'm not clear what you mean by the word "resurrection" anyway.' In this chapter, we'll be looking at some of the genuine difficulties people have with the resurrection of Jesus Christ, and how you can help them with these.

It was easy for first-century Jews to believe in a resurrection

'Look,' your friend might say, 'it was easy for those first Christians to accept the idea of Jesus' resurrection. They lived in the first century. They expected things like resurrections to happen. My problem is that I live two thousand years later, when we just don't expect things like that to happen. I find it very difficult to accept, I'm afraid.' Now this is a perfectly understandable difficulty. In response, you can argue along two lines. First, your friend is wrong about first-century Jewish beliefs. Secondly, the behaviour of the disciples around the time of the crucifixion clearly indicates that they weren't expecting Jesus to be raised from the dead so soon afterwards.

Jewish beliefs about the resurrection

Your friend is actually wrong on one crucial point – those first-century Christians didn't expect Jesus to be raised at all. Perhaps they ought to have expected this. After all, Jesus foretold his coming death and resurrection as he and his disciples went up to Jerusalem for the last time (see Mark 8:31; 9:31–32). Nevertheless, the idea of someone being raised from the dead here and now – in human history! – was outrageous at the time! One widespread expectation was that people would be raised from the dead at the end of time – on the 'last day'. Look at John 11:23–24. Martha summarizes this resurrection expectation very neatly: it is something which happens at the end of time – not something which could happen there and then. However, others at the time, such as the Sadducees, denied any resurrection altogether (Mark 12:18; Acts 23:8).

After two thousand years, Christians have got used to the idea of Jesus being raised from the dead – but the idea is actually very strange. Indeed, by the standards of the first century, it was an extraordinary belief. It was totally different from the two opinions in general circulation – that there was no resurrection, or that there would be a general resurrection right at the end of time. Paul was able to exploit the differences between the Pharisees and Sadducees on this point during an awkward moment in his career (see Acts 23:6–8). But this belief concerned the future resurrection of the dead, at the end of time itself. The idea of somebody being raised from the dead, here and now, and appearing to witnesses, was unheard of.

The Christian claim was that Jesus had been raised now, before the end of time. When Paul refers to Jesus as the 'firstfruits' of the resurrection (1 Corinthians 15:20–23), he means that he was the first of many to rise from the dead – but that Jesus had, indeed, been raised before anyone else. This is quite different from Jewish ideas about the resurrection. So there was something quite distinct and unusual about the Christian claim that Jesus had been raised from the dead, which makes it rather difficult to account for.

Why should all the first Christians have adopted a belief which was so strange by the standards of their time? The first Christians simply didn't adopt a wide-spread Jewish belief, as some have suggested – they altered it dramatically. What the Jews thought could only happen at the end of the world was recognized to have happened in human history, before the end of time, and to have been seen and witnessed to by many. This is a startlingly new belief, and its very novelty raises the question of where it came from. Why did the first Christians adopt this belief? The event of the resurrection of Jesus, it would seem, caused them to *break with* (not echo!) the traditional beliefs concerning the resurrection. Neither of the two contemporary beliefs of the time bear any resemblance to the resurrection of Jesus.

It is too easy to overlook how strange the Christian proclamation of the resurrection of Jesus seemed in the first century. The unthinkable appeared to have happened, and for that very reason demanded careful attention. Far from merely fitting into the popular expectation of the pattern of resurrection, what happened to Jesus actually contradicted it. The sheer novelty of the Christian position at the time has been obscured by two thousand years' experience of the Christian understanding of the resurrection – yet at the time it was wildly unorthodox.

The disciples did not expect Jesus to be raised

This point about the *unexpectedness* of Jesus' resurrection is confirmed by the behaviour of the disciples around the time of the crucifixion. It is obvious from the gospel accounts of the crucifixion of Jesus that the first disciples thought that this was the end of everything. The man who they had given up everything to follow was executed. The men who executed him were professionals: to suggest that they made a botched job of killing Jesus (so that Jesus revived in the tomb) is terribly implausible. We can feel a profound sense of sadness as we read those gospel accounts. The disciples slink away, demoralized and dispirited. They give every impression of being hopeless and helpless, like sheep without a shepherd.

Then suddenly all this changes. A band of sad, demoralized cowards is transformed into a joyful group of potential martyrs, for whom death no longer held any terror. Something which they didn't expect has obviously happened. How else can we account for this remarkable transformation? A mass delusion, perhaps? Hypnosis? The alternatives are certainly there but they lack plausibility. As Pinchas Lapide, a leading Orthodox Jewish scholar, has perceptively remarked in his work *The Resurrection of Jesus*, 'without the resurrection of Jesus, after Golgotha, there would not have been any Christianity'. Lapide notes particularly the new mood of the disciples:

> When this scared, frightened band of the apostles which was just about to throw away everything in order to flee in despair to Galilee; when these peasants, shepherds and fishermen, who betrayed and denied their master and then failed him miserably, suddenly could be changed into a confident mission society, convinced of salvation and able to work with much more success after

Easter than before Easter, then no vision or hallucination is sufficient to explain such a revolutionary transformation.

Let's illustrate this further by looking at Peter, the man who failed Jesus when the going got tough. When Peter seemed to be in personal danger through being associated with Jesus before the resurrection, he denied having anything to do with him (Mark 14:66–72). But, as far as we know, Peter was martyred at Rome for his faith after the resurrection (John 21:18–19 refers to this). The change is obvious and remarkable. What has caused Peter to abandon his fear of death? Perhaps the finest answer to this question is provided by Peter himself: it is the 'new birth into a living hope through the resurrection of Jesus Christ from the dead' (1 Peter 1:3).

Throughout the New Testament, we find that the theme of victory over death is proclaimed with great enthusiasm. It was something relevant, exciting and liberating. Christians need not fear persecution nor death itself, because death has been defeated through the resurrection of Jesus. Now it is *possible* that the first Christians were a crowd of deluded idiots, who were prepared to be martyred for a myth – but somehow, it all seems terribly implausible. It is obvious that something totally unexpected happened to Jesus and that this transformed the situation of those first Christians.

Before his death, Jesus spoke to his disciples about the future. He told them that he would suffer, be rejected, be killed and that finally he would be raised again after three days (Mark 8:31). He told them that, after his death and resurrection, he would go before them to Galilee (Mark 14:28). It seems that the disciples found these words difficult to understand. 'Being raised again' – what could that mean? After all, everyone would be raised on the last day. How could Jesus talk about being raised again and then going to Galilee? It just didn't make sense.

Now when the disciples were faced with the empty tomb, it seems as if scales suddenly fell from their eyes, as they realized that these words were being fulfilled. Suddenly they seem to have realized that Jesus wasn't talking about a resurrection right at the end of time, but here and now – on the third day. Suddenly, all the pieces of the jigsaw seem to have come together, giving a picture of Jesus' resurrection which differed completely from anything they had expected!

All the evidence indicates that the disciples were not expecting Jesus to be raised – hence their initial amazement and fright, and their subsequent joy, as they realized what must have happened. Once more, we find clear evidence for the unexpectedness of Jesus' resurrection.

So the suggestion that it was easy for the first Christians to believe in Jesus' resurrection because they were expecting something of the sort is based upon a misunderstanding. You should have little difficulty in explaining this along the lines suggested.

All this nonsense about the resurrection makes a simple gospel complicated

'Look,' your friend might say, 'it seems to me that Christianity is basically about the teaching of Jesus. In other words, Jesus is a good teacher, like Mohammed or Socrates. Now that I can accept. But why do you go and make this simple gospel so complicated by all this nonsense about the resurrection? It makes Christianity much more difficult to accept!'

Once more, this is an important objection. It must be taken seriously, partly because it reflects a serious misunderstanding about what Christianity really is. Your basic answer, which we will justify in a moment, would be something like this. 'Well, I believe in the resurrection because it seems to me that there is no other way of explaining the evidence. I can understand your difficulty, but I think the only criterion we can use here is not whether it is *easy to believe*, or whether it's *simple*, but whether it is *right*. If it *is* right, then the idea that Jesus is just a good teacher (like Socrates) has to be abandoned as inadequate. It just doesn't take account of what the resurrection means. The resurrection places Jesus in a unique category: there's never been anyone like him before, and there never will be again. He's unique and the reason why he's unique is that the resurrection proves that he's the Son of God.'

Now there's a lot in that response, all of which is important. Let's look at the points.

1. The real question is whether the resurrection really happened, not whether it makes Christianity complicated!

2. If the resurrection took place, it establishes Jesus as unique. There is something very special about him, which sets him apart from everyone else who has ever lived.

3. If the resurrection took place, Jesus is far more than a good religious or moral teacher: he's the Son of God.

4. Simplicity is one thing; truth, however, is quite another! As C. S. Lewis pointed out, the really simple religions are actually those *invented* by human beings.

What is the New Testament evidence for the resurrection of Jesus?

The main lines of evidence from within the New Testament for the resurrection of Jesus are the following.

The tomb was empty

Each of the four gospels tells us that the tomb in which Jesus' body was laid on the Friday evening was empty on the Sunday morning (Matthew 28:1–10; Mark 16:1–8; Luke 24:1–11; John 20:1–9). There is a certain degree of difference between the four accounts on minor points. Was the tomb to be discovered just *before* dawn (Matthew and John), or just *after* dawn (Mark)? Matthew, Luke and John mention that the women, after realizing that the tomb was empty, told the other disciples; Mark, however, makes no mention of this fact. Yet all the gospels insist upon a core of hard historical fact:

1. The tomb was empty.
2. Jesus appeared to his disciples and others after his death.
3. The Jewish authorities couldn't disprove the Christian claim that Jesus had been raised from the dead.

Variation on minor points of detail is a characteristic feature of eyewitness reports. If you ever listen to witnesses in a courtroom, you will very often be amazed by the different way in which they describe the same event. They may all be able to agree on what happened, and when. But on minor points of detail (for example, what happened immediately before or after that event), they very often differ. An event is experienced differently by various people. Major agreement is accompanied by minor disagreement.

Look at the way in which the same events are reported by different news networks on television, for example. Minor discrepancies in details of eyewitness reports actually point to their authenticity, not their inauthenticity. If the gospel accounts of the resurrection were based upon an invention, we would have expected their minor disagreements to have been removed before publication! Let's take this point a little bit further.

Critics of the New Testament resurrection accounts often seem to apply one set of standards to the New Testament, and a totally different set to their everyday existence. For example, if the *Washington Post* and *New York Times* reported the same story in slightly different terms, hardly anyone (except a New Testament critic who applied his standards consistently!) would dream of suggesting that one had copied the other. Similarities between the stories would be held to arise from the event they were reporting.

It is only in the world of New Testament criticism that stories are never derived from events, but simply from other people's versions of that story. And nobody would draw the ridiculous conclusion that, because their accounts were so similar, the event they reported could not have happened! The world of New Testament critics sometimes seems to be one in which similarities between reports of an event is enough to allow them to conclude that the event did not happen.

Let's suppose that all four gospels reported *exactly* the same pattern of events on that first Easter Day perhaps down to using the same words. Would that make them more credible to a critic? Certainly not! He would immediately argue that they were fabrications. They were cooked up. He would suggest that the accounts had been 'doctored' to bring them into line with each other! He would dismiss them as crude forgeries. On the other hand, if they differed wildly from each other, the same critic could dismiss them with equally great ease but for different reasons. He would argue that they weren't talking about the same thing. He would suggest that it was impossible to gain any impression of what had really happened. He would dismiss them as having no importance in assessing the claim that Jesus Christ had been raised from the dead.

So, totally different or totally identical accounts would be dismissed by such a critic. What, then, would such a critic accept as reliable? The answer can only be accounts which vary on minor points, but are agreed upon the central point of importance – which is exactly what we find in the gospel accounts of the discovery of the empty tomb! All agree that the tomb was discovered to be empty early on that Sunday morning, and that there was universal astonishment at this event (which, of course, further backs up the suggestion that they weren't expecting a resurrection).

Another point is of importance here. In Matthew 23:29–30 we find reference to the practice of 'tomb veneration'. When a prophet or martyr died, his tomb became a place of worship for his followers. Yet the New Testament contains not so much as a hint that Jesus' tomb was venerated. Why should the first Christians not have treated Jesus' tomb with the respect it would normally have been given? There was clearly something *odd* about Jesus' tomb, if we are to account for this unlikely omission. Jesus' tomb never became a place of pilgrimage, or even of interest, to Christians. And the empty tomb accounts for this omission with ease: as Jesus was raised from the dead, there was no point in venerating his tomb! He wasn't there any more.

Of course, a critic might say, this is all very well but you've just been talking about the gospels. What about Paul? We don't find any reference to an empty tomb in Paul's writings, do we? The critic is, of course, right, in that there is no *explicit* reference to the empty tomb in any of the letters of Paul. But so what? Why should we expect to find any such reference in Paul's writings? Let's make three points.

1. As mentioned earlier, Paul is writing *letters*, not accounts of the life, death and resurrection of Jesus Christ! When I write letters to Christian friends about the faith we have in common, I concentrate upon the relevance of the risen Christ for our lives. That is exactly what Paul does.

He has no need to talk about the empty tomb.

2. Paul was not a witness to the empty tomb. He could certainly witness to the power of the resurrection to transform his life – but not to something which he had not seen personally. Equally, his witness to the resurrection of Jesus rested upon his personal experience (1 Corinthians 15:8).

3. Paul's letters tend to deal with matters on which he and those he was writing to *disagreed*. Usually, Paul has to intervene to settle some dispute or other. He has no need to dwell on matters on which they agree (although he occasionally does). The empty tomb was not a matter of disagreement among the first Christians, and Paul simply has no need to refer to it. Paul never refers to the fact that Jesus taught in parables. He never refers to the fact that Jesus was condemned before Pontius Pilate. He doesn't need to! But this doesn't allow us to conclude that Jesus *didn't* teach in parables, or that he *wasn't* condemned before Pontius Pilate. The argument from Paul's silence on the matter overlooks both the nature of Paul's writings, and the reason why he wrote them in the first place!

However, Paul's emphasis upon the resurrection in his writings is beyond dispute. While still a persecutor of the Christians, Paul encountered the risen Lord on the road to Damascus (see Acts 9:1–9; 22:4–16; 26:9–18; Galatians 1:11–16). His faith ultimately depended upon that encounter with the risen Lord – how could he doubt that he was risen? Indeed, he often spoke of the 'power of the resurrection' (Philippians 3:10). And there were others who had shared the same experience. Paul mentions that there were more than five hundred witnesses to this experience (1 Corinthians 15:5–7), many of whom were still living twenty-five years after the resurrection. And it was the resurrection which convinced Paul that Jesus really was the long-awaited Messiah (Romans 1:3–4). In short: the evidence is that the tomb was empty. The question which had to be answered was simply this: why?

The corpse of Jesus could not be accounted for

It is of the greatest importance that the New Testament does not contain so much as the slightest trace of an attempt to reconcile belief in Jesus' resurrection with the existence of his corpse in some Palestinian grave. Nor is there any hint – in the New Testament, or anywhere else – that the Jewish authorities either produced, or attempted to produce, the corpse of Jesus. Had this been done, the preaching of the early church would have been discredited immediately. Was there no enemy of the first Christians who could have destroyed their preaching of the resurrection by that one, simple and dramatic act – the production of the body?

But the intriguing fact remains that no such move was made to discredit the first Christians' proclamation of the resurrection and its implications – and the simplest explanation of this remarkable omission is that the corpse was disquietingly absent from its tomb. All the evidence indicates that the tomb was empty on the third day. The controversy at the time concerned not the *fact* of the empty tomb, but the *explanation* of that emptiness. Matthew records one explanation advanced by one group of critics of Jesus – the disciples had stolen the body at night (Matthew 28:13–15). But it is clear that the disciples believed in a somewhat more exciting explanation – that Jesus had been raised from the dead.

Once more, we must emphasize this point: there can be no doubt that the first disciples did believe that Jesus had been raised by God. The reports concerning the empty tomb are completely consistent with this belief, and must be regarded as being at least as historically plausible as any report of any event from the time. Our task is simply to account for this belief, and ask whether it is likely to be correct.

It would have been a simple matter to discredit the Christian message. It could have been done at a stroke. All that was needed was one corpse. The Christian message could not have survived if the dead body of Jesus was placed on public display in Jerusalem. The Christian assertion that Jesus had been raised from the dead was potentially very threatening to two groups of people – the Jews and the Romans. It was in the interests of both to discredit this assertion immediately if they could. But they couldn't, and they didn't. Why not? All the evidence points to the disconcerting fact that Jesus' corpse could not be found.

Jesus was worshipped as God

The next point which must be considered is the remarkably exalted understandings of Jesus which became widespread within Christian circles within a surprisingly short period after his death. As we have already seen, Jesus was not venerated as a dead prophet or rabbi – he was worshipped as the living and risen Lord. At some points in the New Testament, as we noted in the previous chapter, Jesus appears to be explicitly identified with God himself, and some sort of implicit identification along these lines is widespread, and would become normative in the following centuries. In his letter to Trajan, which we also noted in the previous chapter (p. 50), Pliny refers to the Christian practice of singing hymns to Jesus as God.

Furthermore, as we saw earlier (pp. 57–59), at several points in the New Testament, words originally referring to God himself are applied to Jesus. Two examples are especially interesting. In Romans 10:13, Paul states that 'everyone who calls on the name of the Lord [Jesus, in this

77

case] will be saved' – yet the original of this Old Testament quotation (Joel 2:32) is actually a statement to the effect that everyone who calls upon the name of God will be saved. In Philippians 2:10, Paul alters an Old Testament prophecy to the effect that everyone will one day bow at the name of God (Isaiah 45:23) to refer to Jesus.

But how could this remarkable transformation in the perceived status of Jesus have come about? He died as a common criminal, perhaps even a prophet, or maybe a martyr – but the most this would merit would be veneration of his tomb (see Matthew 23:29). Of course, we have already noted that there was a problem about Jesus' tomb, which was found to be empty so soon after his death. But the point still remains important: why did the early Christians start talking about a dead rabbi as if he were God? And, perhaps even more interesting, why did they start talking about him as if he were alive, praying to him, and worshipping him?

Once more, we must note that it is possible that they were the victims of a hysterical delusion which has continued to this day. Yet there is another far more convincing explanation – that they believed that Jesus had been raised from the dead by God, thus establishing or demonstrating the unique relationship between God and Jesus. And it was on the basis of their understanding of this unique relationship that the early Christians based their views of Jesus.

Your friends may well have the idea that Christians look to Jesus as a teacher in much the same way as Marxists look to Marx. But, as we saw in the last chapter, this just isn't right! You need to explain to them that Christians don't treat Jesus as a dead figure from the past who had some interesting ideas. They worship him as the living Lord. Jesus isn't treated as a dead rabbi – even a super-rabbi! – but as someone who is present, who is *alive*, who can meet us here and now.

Can the resurrection can be explained on purely rational grounds?

'Surely,' your friend might say, 'we can explain the resurrection accounts of the New Testament in other ways. The idea of Jesus being raised from the dead is difficult for me to accept. There must be a simpler explanation of what happened. Maybe there was some misunderstanding on the part of the disciples. Perhaps they were dishonest. Or maybe they were just deluded idiots, who got confused about what happened.'

The main alternative explanations of the resurrection accounts of the New Testament are the following.

1. Jesus didn't really die at all on the cross – he just fainted, and later he revived.

2. The first Christians 'borrowed' pagan myths about dying and rising gods.

Let's look at these individually.

Jesus didn't really die upon the cross

Is it really likely that experienced Roman executioners would have botched up Jesus' execution? Would they have been likely to confuse fainting and dying? Some nineteenth-century rationalists certainly thought so, and their ideas have even found their way into more recent discussions of the subject. Here's the theory that one of them – H. E. G. Paulus, writing in 1828 – put forward.

In first-century Palestine, it was quite common for people to be buried when they weren't actually dead. This is exactly what happened with Jesus. He fainted on the cross. Now it is true, as Paulus concedes, that Jesus was stabbed with a spear before he was taken down from the cross (see John 19:34). But Paulus is well versed in the latest medical theory (in 1828 that is). He knows that one way to make someone recover is to bleed them. So what really happened was that the spear didn't penetrate Jesus' heart, but simply cut a vein. The loss of blood then helped him recover from his trance.

Jesus' body was then taken to a grave. The smell of the spices in which he was wrapped, and the coolness of the tomb, combined to revive him. So, on the Sunday morning, he was able to leave the tomb. Fortunately, the great stone which had blocked the entrance had been moved by an earthquake, so he was able to get out without too much difficulty. Nearby, he managed to find a set of gardener's clothes, which he put on (and, of course, Mary then mistook him for a gardener: John 20:15). After that, Jesus put in the occasional appearance to his disciples. These disciples, of course, being unsophisticated and backward peasants, thought that he was risen from the dead. After forty days, however, he realized that he was finally going to die from his wounds. So he climbed a nearby mountain to say goodbye to his followers. A cloud then appears from somewhere, so that Jesus disappears from view. Then Jesus went off somewhere – nobody knows where – never to be heard of again, and died.

Without wishing to seem disrespectful, this seems very difficult to take seriously. The possibility that a group of professional Roman executioners should have failed in their task is improbable enough. The reference to 'blood and water' when Jesus' side was pierced after the crucifixion (John 19:34) would seem to be a reference to the *post mortem* separation of the blood into clot and serum, indicating that Jesus was unequivocally dead. As this presumably wasn't a known medical fact when John's gospel was written, it is unlikely to have been included to make the account seem more plausible. We are also being asked to believe that this hungry, thirsty and seriously wounded man would have been able to unwind his grave-clothes and crawl from his tomb. And not only that, but we are being asked to believe that he would have given his disciples the impression that he was the conqueror over death, when in fact he was obviously a seriously ill man who would die of his wounds shortly afterwards!

Now it is possible that someone who is deliberately determined not to believe in the resurrection may find this a convincing explanation. Even many critics of Christianity, however, find it totally implausible, saying little for the credibility of those who suggest it. It is just not an adequate explanation.

The resurrection is based on a myth

This is a more subtle and sophisticated objection, which you are much less likely to meet. However, you may come across it, in which case it is important that you know what to say in response. If your friend is into ancient Egyptian mythology, he might well suggest that the idea of dying and rising gods was commonplace in the ancient world. Gods such as Attis, Adonis, Isis and Serapis were originally vegetation deities. The Egyptians, noticing that vegetation kept disappearing in winter and reappearing in spring, developed the idea that there was some sort of vegetation god who spent six months on high and six months on earth. Later, under the influence of Greek thought, these gods came to be thought of as dying and rising again, in a yearly cycle. So, your friend might argue, all that Christians have done is to hijack these myths. They have taken the idea of a god who dies and rises again, and based the idea of the resurrection upon it.

This suggestion might well have been taken very seriously between about 1890 and 1930. Since then, however, scholarship has moved on considerably. The parallels between the pagan myths of dying and rising gods and the New Testament accounts of the resurrection of Jesus are now regarded as remote, to say the least. For instance, the New Testament documents record with some care the place and the date of both the death and the resurrection of Jesus, as well as identifying the witnesses to both. The contrast with the ahistorical narrative form of mythology is striking. *When* did Attis die? *Where* did he die? *Who* saw it happen? *When* did he rise again? *Where* did he rise again? *Who* were the witnesses to this alleged 'resurrection'? The New Testament gives us answers to all six of these questions. It treats the resurrection as a definite historical event. But the 'dying-and-rising-god' myth makes no claim to be based in historical reality.

Furthermore, there are no known instances of this myth being applied to any *specific historical figure* in pagan literature, so that the New Testament writers would have given a stunningly original twist to this mythology. It is at this point that the wisdom of the great literary scholar C. S. Lewis – who actually knew something about myths – must be acknowledged. Lewis realized that the New Testament accounts of the resurrection of Jesus bore no relation to real mythology, despite the protests of some theologians who had dabbled in the field in a thoroughly amateur fashion.

Another theory which was in fashion in the 1930s was that Christians took over what are sometimes known as 'gnostic redeemer myths', which also spoke of a dying and rising saviour god. Since about 1950, however, it has been generally accepted that the gnostic redeemer myths – which the New Testament writers allegedly took over and applied to Jesus – were to be dated from later than the New Testament itself. The gnostics, it seems, actually took over Christian ideas! Anyway, there is no evidence whatsoever that the first Christians knew anything about Egyptian mythology. How could Christians adapt something of which they knew nothing? The first people to proclaim the resurrection of Jesus were mostly Jewish peasants, who would hardly have come across such sophisticated foreign mythological speculation.

The idea that the resurrection is based upon some ancient Eastern myth is not taken with any degree of seriousness in scholarly circles today. You may still, of course, find the occasional student who has read some influential book from the 1920s – like J. G. Frazer's *Adonis, Attis, Isiris* – and takes its ideas seriously. But scholarship has moved on since then! Whatever the resurrection may be, it isn't a re-hashed Egyptian myth!

Dead people don't rise again

'But', your friend may say, 'surely I am right to exclude the possibility of the resurrection. Dead men don't rise. Jesus was a man. Therefore Jesus cannot have risen from the dead – and that's all there is to it. There is just no point in arguing about the evidence – because you can't have evidence for something which is an impossibility!'

This objection picks up some themes developed by the eighteenth-century Scottish philosopher David Hume. Hume argued that you needed contemporary analogues for events like the resurrection. In other words, you need to be able to point to comparable events in the present before you can believe in the resurrection. Because we don't see dead men or women rising from the dead today, Hume argued, we have reason to call into question whether Jesus rose from the dead in the first century.

This argument sounds convincing, until we begin to look at it more closely. Let's suppose that about one person in a thousand rose from the dead on a more or less regular basis. It's a common occurrence. We've all seen it happen. The idea doesn't present any difficulties for us. And so we would have no difficulty in accepting that Jesus rose from the dead in the first century.

But if this was the case, we would not have any interest in Jesus! Jesus would simply be yet another example of something we all know from experience. He wouldn't be special. His resurrection wouldn't be *important*. The fact that he was raised from the dead wouldn't distinguish him from all others.

Now the simple fact is that Christians have always insisted that Jesus was unique – that he was singled out from all others by the fact that he, and he alone, was raised from the dead in history. There will be a general resurrection at the end of time, certainly – but Jesus is the only person ever to have been raised from the dead in human history. Lazarus was brought back to life, only to die again. The resurrection of Jesus is totally different. He is the firstfruits from the dead (1 Corinthians 15:20). In other words, his resurrection is unique, and without any parallel in human history. This obviously raises a difficulty. If – as Christians have always insisted is the case – Jesus' resurrection is unique, then by definition there can't be any other occurrences of the same event. If there were other occurrences, it would certainly make it a lot easier to believe in Jesus' resurrection – but his resurrection would no longer have the crucial importance which Christians attach to it.

The fact that there are no other persons who have been raised from the dead may well make it more difficult to accept that Jesus was raised – but it also underscores Jesus' uniqueness. He, and he alone, was singled out in this way. He was not merely special – he was unique. What is it that distinguishes Jesus from Socrates, Mohammed or Gandhi? None but Jesus was raised from the dead by God – and it is *this* which leads us to take

Jesus' teaching with the seriousness it deserves. After all, if you suspect that you are dealing with the Son of God, you will take his teaching more seriously than you might otherwise! For the New Testament, Jesus' resurrection clinches his identity – it proves that he was the Son of God (Romans 1:3–4 is worth noting here). It is the key to his identity and relevance.

In this chapter, we've been looking at some of the main objections which might be raised by your friends against the resurrection of Jesus. None of them is fatal. By helping them to see this, you may be able to remove obstacles which prevent them from encountering the risen Christ. That encounter itself is the final proof of the resurrection!

6

Salvation

One of the great themes of the New Testament is that God has made available and possible a new life and a new hope through the death and resurrection of Jesus Christ. The full exploration of this theme is linked with the doctrine of salvation, which aims to establish what salvation is, and how it is possible through the death and resurrection of Christ. A full discussion of its many facets lies beyond us, but it will be enormously helpful to the reader to take time to explore what God was doing on the cross, using some of the books recommended at the end of this book. In this chapter, we shall explore a number of specific difficulties people have in thinking and talking about salvation which need careful consideration. The present chapter will deal with four major problem areas, focusing on the nature of salvation, and how it relates to us.

What is salvation?

For many people, the very idea of salvation is something of a problem. 'What do you mean by "salvation"?' they may ask. 'What does it mean to be saved?' It is very helpful to be able to explain the various ways in which Scripture describes salvation, in order to help people get a 'feel' for what it is like. The biblical understanding of what Jesus Christ achieved upon the cross is remarkably rich and profound. It can challenge and excite people – but it needs to be *explained*.

So far in this book, we've been looking at ways in which you can defend Christianity against objections. In this chapter, we're mainly concerned with explaining what Christianity has to say on the great question of the relevance of the death of Jesus Christ for the human race. Let us begin by explaining how Christians understand what 'salvation' actually means.

The New Testament uses a number of ideas to explain what Jesus Christ achieved on the cross. So deep and rich is the Christian understanding of what he achieved, that no one single idea can capture it in its totality. So the New Testament uses a series of ideas and images to describe it. Just as a group of jigsaw pieces build up to disclose an overall picture (which no single piece can disclose by itself), so these ideas and images build up to give us a full understanding of what Jesus achieved on the cross. Let's look at the main ones and see how you might explain them.

Salvation

The very name 'Jesus' means 'God saves' (see Matthew 1:21), showing how important the idea of 'being saved' or 'salvation' is within the New Testament. What does it mean? The Greek word used (*soteria*) has two main meanings, each of which is very helpful in explaining the relevance of Jesus Christ's death and resurrection for us.

1. It means 'being rescued', or 'being delivered from a dangerous situation'. For example, you might be in prison, or held captive by a foreign power (just as Israel was held captive in Egypt). When you are 'saved', you are set free from bondage. You are liberated. Human beings are held captive by the power of sin and by the fear of

death. These are forces which have enormous influence over our lives. Christ came to die and rise again in order to release us from these forces. He came that we might have life in all its fullness, through breaking the power of sin and death over us.

2. It means 'making whole' or 'restoring'. If you compare some translations of the New Testament, you'll find that Mark 5:34 is sometimes translated as 'your faith has saved you' and sometimes as 'your faith has made you whole'. There is a very close connection between the ideas of 'salvation' and 'wholeness' or 'healing'. For the Christian, 'salvation' includes the very important idea of 'being restored to wholeness'. Through Christ's death and resurrection, we are offered the possibility of being fulfilled as persons.

Our potential as human beings can only be fully realized when we come to enter into a relationship with God, a relationship which is now broken. The French philosopher Pascal remarked that 'there is a God-shaped gap within us' – meaning that we are incomplete until we relate to God. The story of creation in Genesis (Genesis 1:26–27) emphasizes that God created us in his image and likeness – in other words, with the capacity to relate to him.

The cross and resurrection of Jesus opens up the possibility of being restored to the fullness of our relationship with God. We are made whole again by being restored to fellowship with God. Salvation is about being rescued from the power of sin which alienates us from God, and from the fear of death which is the result of sin. It is about being restored to fellowship with the living and loving God.

Many people are concerned about the 'human potential' – in other words, about how to live fully as human beings. Even secular humanists regard this as an important question. It is important that the Christian contribution to this discussion should be heard. For Christianity is also about fulfilling the human potential, although the solution it provides will differ from that of secular humanism. The gospel proclaims that Jesus Christ came in order that we might have life in all its fullness, by opening the way to restoring us to fellowship with God. That fullness, of course, has both personal and social implications: Christians must never behave as if salvation is simply concerned with individual believers: God has a vision for the salvation, the making whole, of society as well.

This point about the social dimension of salvation is important. Critics of Christianity often suggest that it's just about 'pie in the sky when you die'. In other words, it's just about saving individuals. The scriptural idea of 'salvation', however, takes in two major themes: first, restoring the individual to fellowship with God, and second, restoring human society to what God wishes it to be. It's about the restoration of both human beings and society to what God intended them to be. 'Restoring the kingdom' embraces both individual and society. To suggest that the Christian gospel is just about saving individual souls is a serious distortion of what Christianity is about. Christianity has a great social vision, which its critics often manage to overlook, even though Christians have been in the forefront of many great social reforming movements.

So in what ways do Christians differ from secular social reforming movements? Perhaps most importantly, they differ in their understanding of human nature. The idea of 'original sin', to be discussed shortly, points to there being something deeply flawed in human nature. Many secular ideologies, such as Marxism, argue that there is something wrong simply with *society*: change society, and all will be well. The Christian suggests that there is something inherently flawed in human nature, which is reflected in the way society has developed. It is human nature, as much as society, which needs to be restored. The Christian vision is comprehensive: both individuals and society need restoration to wholeness.

Reconciliation and forgiveness

Many of the ideas used by the New Testament to unpack the relevance of the death and resurrection of Jesus Christ – including the two we're going to look at now – are based upon personal relationships. The parable traditionally referred to as the 'parable of the prodigal son' (Luke 15:11–32) is perhaps one of the best-known passages of Scripture. It is an ideal starting-point for explaining the ideas of 'reconciliation' and 'forgiveness' to your friends. It is a powerful way of beginning to explore the meaning of the death and resurrection of Jesus Christ. The parable tells of a son who chooses to turn his back on his father, and gain his independence in 'a distant country'. Having spent all his money (the word 'prodigal' means 'wasteful'), he finds that he longs to be restored to his father.

At the heart of the parable is the transformation of a personal relationship – a personal relationship which has gone wrong. The parable tells us of how the son becomes alienated from his father. He decides to go his own way, into the 'distant country' (Luke 15:13). While he is far from his father, he realizes just how much the relationship meant to him. He decides to return home, and ask for his father's forgiveness. So he begins the long journey home, wondering how his father will react to his homecoming. When he is still far away from home, his father sees him and runs to meet him. He has been waiting for him! The rejoicing begins.

This beautifully illuminates the situation in which many young people find themselves. Like the son in the parable, they have wandered into a 'distant country', where they thought they would be free and happy. Yet life without God so often seems meaningless and unsatisfying. The distant country seems very attractive, seen from far away – but once they get there, they find it fails to meet up to expectations. They long to return home. Every day and age has its own special 'distant country'. For one generation, it may be the seductive delusion of a Marxist utopia; for another, the mysteries of a half-understood Eastern religion; for a third, narcotics. Each seems attractive. They seem exciting and new, compared with the constancy of Christianity. And then the dreadful moment comes, when the illusion has to be faced for what it really is. Perhaps then they begin to think about God. Is he there? Is he interested in them? Would he be prepared to have them back?

It is questions such as these that the ideas of 'reconciliation' and 'forgiveness' begin to deal with. The New Testament tells us that our relationship with God is rather like other personal relationships. All of us are involved in personal relationships of one sort or another, and can immediately understand the gospel proclamation when it's presented in these terms. Let's suppose that two people (let's call them 'Paul' and 'Elizabeth') develop a relationship. They come to mean a lot to each other. Then imagine that Elizabeth does something to offend Paul. Perhaps Elizabeth doesn't even realize that Paul has been offended. But the relationship goes wrong. Paul and Elizabeth become alienated from each other. The relationship is in ruins.

Then Paul decides to do something about the situation by talking to Elizabeth, and confronting the painful fact that the relationship has gone wrong. He will explain how much the relationship means to him, and offer to forgive her. This means that Elizabeth will have to admit that she has hurt Paul, and face up to all the pain and hurt it has caused – but having done this, the relationship is restored. Paul and Elizabeth are reconciled to each other.

You could use analogies like these to begin to explain the cross to your friends. The New Testament tells us that God takes the initiative in trying to restore our relationship with him. The full extent of our separation from him is shown. We realize that we, like the wasteful son, are in a 'distant country', far from God. We realize that we are sinners. And then we begin to appreciate the full extent of God's love for us, as we realize that the Son of God died for us upon the cross (John 3:16; Romans 5:8; Galatians 2:20). God deals with the objective reality of sin through his death on the cross, breaking its stranglehold upon us. The death of Jesus Christ upon the cross demonstrates the reality of our sin and the full extent of our separation from God – and at the same time speaks to us of the overwhelming tender love of God for us. We realize how much we mean to God. And then perhaps we feel moved to do something about it.

The cross speaks to us of reconciliation and forgiveness. For Paul, 'God was reconciling the world to himself in Christ' (2 Corinthians 5:19). Elsewhere, he uses the same word to refer to the reconciliation of a husband and wife whose relationship has broken down (1 Corinthians 7:11). Through the death and resurrection of Jesus Christ, God makes it possible for us to be reconciled to him. Our relationship with him can be transformed. All the obstacles to that relationship have been removed by God. One only remains – our reluctance to repent, to say 'yes' to his offer of forgiveness. God may seem far away and distant – but that can change, and change very suddenly. He is offering us forgiveness, allowing us to set the past behind us, so that we may go forward with him into eternal life.

Justification

For Paul, Christians have been 'justified through faith' (Romans 5:1). But what does the word 'justification' mean? For some people, 'justification' is something you do to right-hand margins on word processors – it hasn't got anything obvious to do with God! However, the word has the basic meaning of 'putting in the right'. Sin is a wrong relationship with God – but faith is a right relationship with God. To be 'justified' means that we are placed in a right relationship with God – or, to put it another way, we are made 'right with God' through the death and resurrection of Jesus. The guilt of our sin is thus cancelled as a result of the obedience of Christ.

What is sin?

The word 'sin' itself can cause considerable difficulty for some people. Many people have problems with Christianity because they don't understand what 'sin' actually means. They think it has something to do only with sexual morality. It's therefore useful to be able to explain two basic scriptural ways of talking about sin.

Sin as missing the mark

Just as an arrow misses its target by falling short, so we have missed our full relationship with God by falling short of the required standard. 'All have sinned and fall short of the glory of God' (Romans 3:23). Some may come closer to the target than others, but the fact remains that they have still missed it. 'A miss is as good as a mile,' as they say. Some people are much more moral than others – but they still fall short of the required standard.

Sin as rebellion

Deep down in human beings is a desire to go one's own way, to be independent of God. The story of Adam and Eve (Genesis 3:4–6) tells of how Adam decided he wished to be like God, being able to decide what was good and what was evil – in other words, to set himself up in the place of God. And the wasteful son rebels against his father, setting off into the 'distant country' to be independent (see pp. 90–91). Just as children rebel against their parents, so the New Testament speaks of us rebelling against God. We want to live our lives without him.

One of the most poignant passages in Scripture is Hosea 11:1–5. Here God speaks of his overwhelmingly tender love for his people: he brought them out of Egypt and tended them. Yet his people now seem to have forgotten all about him. They want to live their lives without taking any notice of the God who loved them and brought them out of captivity into the promised land. Sin is living one's life without God – and time and time again, Scripture speaks to us of the hurt that this causes to God. After all, God loved the world so much that he sent his only Son to die for us. Imagine the hurt and grief it must cause him to be overlooked. The cross shows how heartbroken God is on account of us. This way of thinking about sin helps us understand the problem of sin (living without God), while also reminding us of the incredible depths of the love of God for us.

A helpful distinction which you can make when explaining Christianity to your friends is between *sin* and *sins*. Sin is like a disease, whose symptoms are sins. In other words, sin is what is wrong with human nature, and sins are the effects of this problem. Christianity is primarily concerned with sin – with the basic problem of human nature. It identifies sin as a force, a power, which exercises influence over us. Before we can stop sinning, its power needs to be broken. It is like an illness which makes us commit sins. Before we can stop sinning, we need to be cured of this illness.

For St Paul, the gospel is about God's intervention to deal with sin. Through the death and resurrection of Jesus Christ, the power of sin is broken. Christ's death and resurrection are like a drug which combats the illness of sin, gradually healing us of its wounds. The gospel deals with the root cause of sins: it doesn't just tell people to stop sinning, but deals with the problem which makes them want to sin in the first place.

Many people find the idea of 'original sin' especially difficult. One way of explaining this idea is particularly helpful. The doctrine of original sin tells us that we are born into the world alienated from God. Or, to put it another way, we are born into the world cut off from God. God seems far away and distant, so distant that he might as well not exist. We don't do something which causes us to be cut off from God, because we are already alienated from him. Perhaps you have read the Nobel Laureate William Golding's earliest novel *Lord of the Flies*, a story about what happens to a group of young boys stranded on a desert island paradise. Yet already within them, the boys have the seeds of the evil which unfolds in the pages of the book. Golding vividly explores what he calls 'the darkness of man's heart', as he shows that there is already some force within us, working for evil, from our youth upwards. *Lord of the Flies* is a very helpful way into a discussion with students of English literature on the problem of original sin and the Christian answer to it.

The doctrine of original sin prevents anyone from thinking that our natural relationship with God is right or good enough. It points to there being something wrong with us – some distortion or bias in our nature, some darkness in the depths of our being which we cannot deal with by ourselves. It tells us just how far we have to go if we are to relate to God properly and have life in all its fullness. It is only when we realize just how far we are from God that we begin to appreciate just what good news the gospel really is. The doctrine of original sin destroys any illusions we may have about our standing before God. To relate to God properly and fully, we need to be born all over again (John 3:3). Our physical birth must be followed by a spiritual birth, if we are to have life in all its fullness.

Earlier, we looked at the biblical idea of 'reconciliation' as one way of unpacking the full meaning of the death and resurrection of Jesus. Sin is about being alienated from God. Like the wasteful son, we are in a 'distant country'. God seems to be far away and remote. Yet the gospel proclaims that we can be reconciled to God – that through the death and resurrection of Jesus Christ, the way back from the 'distant country' to the waiting father has been opened up. Original sin is about alienation from God – just as the gospel is about reconciliation with God through the death and resurrection of Jesus Christ. Original sin is the 'before', and salvation the 'after'.

It is hoped that these brief comments about salvation and sin will help you begin to think of ways of explaining how the death and resurrection of Jesus is of relevance to your friends. We shall return to discuss how you can help them see the relevance of the cross and resurrection soon. First, however, we need to look at a genuine difficulty you may encounter in talking about salvation.

Isn't everyone saved anyway?

This is the position often referred to as 'universal salvation,' or sometimes just 'universalism.' The New Testament often affirms the universal saving will of God. God 'wants all to be saved and to come to a knowledge of the truth' (1 Timothy 2:4). As God wants everyone to be saved, some argue, this proves that everyone eventually will be saved. Why, then, bother talking about Christianity or salvation?

This is an important question and there are a number of answers you can give. For example, it is perfectly obvious that the New Testament works on two basic assumptions: first, that God does indeed want everyone to be saved; second, that not everyone will be saved. The New Testament makes a distinction between those who are going to be saved and those who aren't. A more helpful way of dealing with this question, however, is to get your friend to think through the implications of his suggestion that everyone will be saved.

The gospel affirms the love of God for sinners. Time and time again, we find the New Testament writers exulting in the love of God. Paul asks the Ephesian Christians to try to 'grasp how wide and long and high and deep is the love of Christ' (Ephesians 3:18). But what is love? Love is basically about one person freely offering himself or herself to another. Now as everyone who has ever been in love is only too painfully aware, falling in love with someone doesn't always mean that they automatically fall in love with you! They have a say in whether or not they fall in love with you as well! You can tell them how much you love them. You can do all sorts of things to try and prove how much they mean to you. But in the end, it's a simple fact of life that your offer of love may be turned down. The fact that you love someone doesn't force them into loving you.

Now let's return to God. God loves us. He goes to incredible lengths to show just how much we mean to him. On the cross, we can see the supreme demonstration of the love of God for us – God gave his only Son, so that whoever believes in him should not perish, but have everlasting life (John 3:16). It is clear that God would very much like us to love him as well. Yet we are given the enormous privilege of saying 'no' to God. God does not force himself upon us: he offers himself to us. He knocks at the door of our life, asking us to open the door – but he doesn't break that door down and force his way in. Perhaps you know the famous picture by Holman Hunt, *The Light of the World*. This picture shows Jesus, carrying a lantern, gently knocking at a door, seeking admission from the occupant. He doesn't stand there with a sledgehammer, preparing to smash the door down and gain admission without the occupant's permission!

The gospel proclaims that God loves us, and very much wishes us to accept his offer of love and be saved. But the ball is in our court. God has firmly but courteously done everything he could to gain us our salvation, and he is now offering it to us. But he does not force us to accept his gift. Universalism, however, is obliged to assert that God forces us to be saved.

If all are to be saved, then the possibility of not being saved is excluded. Universalism may well suggest that Jesus knocks at the door of our life, seeking admission – but what happens if we don't want to let him in? Perhaps it is at this point that the sledgehammer is brought out! God may use the velvet glove at first – but the iron fist comes out if we refuse to be saved. And universalism conjures up the most appalling view of God – that of a tyrant, who has no concern whatsoever for the wishes of his creatures. Their God-given freedom is overruled. They *must* be saved, whether they like it or not. This is totally removed from the view of God which we find in the pages of the New Testament.

Christianity asks us to think of a God who loves us so much, that he gave his Son to die for us. Like the father awaiting the return of the wasteful son, he respects the freedom and choice of those whom he loves. Universalism asks us to think of a God who rapes us – who rides roughshod over our wishes, in order to force himself upon us. Unlike the father in the parable, perhaps he sends out troops to recapture the wasteful son, forcing him to return in chains against his will. It is unthinkable and gains no support from the New Testament. God does indeed desire that everyone will be saved – but the New Testament affirms that it is up to us to respond to that offer of salvation. God respects us. Universalism is quite simply sub-Christian, perverting these most precious insights concerning the love of God for sinners.

How is salvation relevant?

The New Testament develops at least three major ways of interpreting the cross and resurrection of Jesus, each of which is charged with enormous relevance for the human situation. You will probably find that at least one of these ways of looking at the cross will challenge your friends.

The cross as the forgiveness of sins

Many people have a deep sense of personal inadequacy and guilt. 'How', they may ask, 'can someone like me ever enter into a relationship with God? After all, he's so holy and righteous, and I am so sinful and insignificant.' This is a very important question, and you need to appreciate that Christianity has a very powerful answer to give.

The cross demonstrates God's determination to deal with human sin. It shows just how serious and costly a thing real forgiveness is – and reassures us that our sins really have been forgiven. God doesn't say something like, 'Never mind, let's pretend that sin doesn't exist.' Instead, God brings together in the cross of Jesus his total condemnation of sin and his tender love for the sinner. We see in the death of Jesus on the cross the full impact of human sin, the full cost of divine forgiveness, and the full extent of the love of God for sinners. God hates the sin and loves the sinner. Christ endured the cross for our sakes, bearing the full penalty that God demands for sin. As a result, sin is forgiven – *really* forgiven. We are able to come to God, as forgiven sinners, as men and women whose sin has been condemned and forgiven. We must learn to accept that we have been accepted by God through the death and resurrection of Christ, despite being unacceptable.

So the cross is indeed good news to those who feel that they cannot possibly come to God on account of their sin or inadequacy. The gospel gloriously affirms that God has forgiven that sin, has overcome that inadequacy. The words of 1 Peter 2:24 are very helpful and important here: 'He himself bore our sins in his body on the tree, so that we might die to sins, and live for righteousness; by his wounds you have been healed.' Through the great events which centred on Calvary, God has wiped out our past sin and, at enormous cost, given us a fresh start. He has smoothed out every difficulty in order that we might go forward with him into eternal life. We are able to turn our backs on our past (which is what the idea of 'repentance' basically means) in order to go forward into the future with the God who loves us.

The cross as victory over death

Many people are frightened of death. Contemporary existentialist philosophers point out how humans try to deny death, try to pretend that they aren't going to die. We like to think that death is something which happens to somebody else. It is very difficult for us to come to terms with the fact that our personal existence will one day be terminated. It is a very threatening and disturbing thought. People are afraid of death. How often has it been said that death is a forbidden subject in the modern world?

It is here that the gospel has a decisive contribution to make. The New Testament points to the death and resurrection of Jesus Christ as God's victory over sin and death (1 Corinthians 15:55–56). Christ 'shared in their humanity so that by his death he might destroy him who holds the power of death – that is, the devil – and free those who all their lives were held in slavery by their fear of death' (Hebrews 2:14–15). The gospel invites those who are afraid of death to look at what God has achieved through the cross and resurrection of Jesus. So long as human beings walk the face of this earth, knowing that they must die, the gospel will continue to be relevant and powerful. We must never lose sight of the relevance and power of the gospel here!

The cross as a demonstration of the love of God

It is natural for us to feel lost in the immensity of the universe. We need to feel loved, to feel that we are important to someone else. Yet at the root of the lives of many, there is a virtual absence of any meaning. President John F. Kennedy once remarked that 'modern American youth has everything – except a reason to live.' And the words of Jean-Paul Sartre express this point with force: 'Here we are, all of us, eating and drinking to preserve our precious existences – and yet there is nothing, nothing, absolutely no reason for existing.' We could even give a name to this feeling of meaninglessness – we could call it an 'existential vacuum'. But that doesn't solve the problem. We still feel lonely and lost, in a vast universe which threatens to overwhelm us.

It is this feeling of meaninglessness which is transformed through the electrifying declaration that God – the same God who created the universe – loves us. Love gives meaning to life, in that the person loved becomes special, assuming a significance which he or she otherwise might not have. Christianity makes the astonishing assertion – which it bases upon the life, death and resurrection of Jesus Christ – that God is profoundly interested in us and concerned for us. We mean something to God; Christ died for us; we are special in the sight of God. Christ came to bring us back from the 'distant country' to our loving and waiting father (but not to force us to go with him, as universalism suggests – only to invite us to accompany him back, if we wish to). In the midst of an immense and frightening universe, we are given meaning and significance by the realization that the God who called the world into being, who created us, also loves us and cares for us, coming down from heaven and going to the cross to prove the full extent of that love to a disbelieving and wondering world.

Why is a response to the gospel necessary?

One final problem remains. Some people find it difficult to understand why we need to respond to God's offer of salvation. They find it difficult to accept that they need to *do something* to enter into a full relationship with the loving and living God. Surely, they might say, it is enough simply to admit the truth of the gospel? It is therefore helpful to be able to explain the need for a response on our part. Four main ways of doing this should be noted.

1. Imagine that someone is offering you a gift. They hold out their hand, and offer you that present. It is there, waiting for you to accept it. But until you reach out and take it, it will not be yours. The offer is genuine – but you must respond to it. As the great theologian John Calvin remarked, faith is like an empty open hand, stretched out towards God, waiting to receive from him. You need to

receive, to accept, the great gift of salvation which God is offering you, if it is to be yours. Faith is basically saying 'Yes!' to God and accepting that salvation and making it our own.

2. Think of the idea of reconciliation. We have already seen how this is an important New Testament way of understanding what God has done for us through the death and resurrection of Jesus Christ. Now imagine that Paul and Elizabeth, who we met earlier, have fallen out again. Their relationship is in ruins. However, Elizabeth decides to restore their relationship. She goes to Paul, and explains how much the relationship means to her. She offers to be reconciled to him, so that their relationship can be restored. What happens if Paul refuses to respond to her offer of reconciliation? The relationship remains ruined. It is only by accepting her offer of reconciliation that the relationship is restored to its fullness. So it is with God. God offers us reconciliation, through the death and resurrection of Jesus Christ. But unless we accept that offer, our relationship with God remains unchanged.

3. Think of the idea of forgiveness. The idea is, of course, central to the gospel. What happens if God offers us forgiveness, yet we refuse to accept it? Is the relationship transformed? To accept an offer of forgiveness is actually quite difficult. It means admitting that we need forgiveness, that we have done something which has hurt someone else. It means having to apologize. The biblical idea of 'repentance' is of central importance: it means acknowledging the hurt we have caused to another, admitting that we are at fault, and humbly asking for forgiveness. But it also means restoring a relationship. Not accepting an offer of forgiveness means that the relationship is unchanged. It is only by accepting God's offer of forgiveness that our relationship with him is transformed. Of course our need for repentance is difficult

for us to admit – for the wasteful son, it meant getting up, going to his father, and saying, 'Father, I have sinned and am no longer worthy to be called your son.' It also means coming home to a loving and waiting God, who rejoices at our return.

4. Think of the gospel as being like a medicine. We have already seen how salvation can be understood as healing. When penicillin was discovered, it was hailed as a wonder drug, capable of curing many illnesses (such as blood poisoning) which had once been fatal. If you had blood poisoning, you could now be cured – provided you took this drug. It could not cure you unless you did this. The gospel is like penicillin. It is capable of transforming our situation. But it must be taken. We need to make a response to the gospel, by applying it. To acknowledge the *truth* of the gospel without responding to it is like saying that penicillin could cure your illness – without taking it! You recognize its potential – but don't benefit from it. A person dying of blood poisoning doesn't gain much from the knowledge that his illness *could* be cured by penicillin – he or she needs to take it, and *be* cured!

All these illustrations make the same point. It is an obvious point but one which some people have genuine difficulty in grasping. You need to accept God's offer of forgiveness. You need to say 'Yes!' to God. You need to apply the gospel. You need to do something. There are, of course, a number of ways of explaining this 'something' to your friends. You may suggest they think of reaching out to receive a precious gift which is being offered to them. You may suggest that they think of accepting an offer of forgiveness. You may suggest that they think of opening a door which leads into their lives (Revelation 3:20). You may suggest that they think of eating the bread of life (John 6:48), or drinking the water which gives eternal life (John 4:13–14).

One of the difficulties in explaining the gospel in very simple terms, as I have tried to do throughout this book, is that there is a danger of over-simplification. It will be obvious that pressure on space has meant that I have not had time to discuss the role of the Holy Spirit in salvation. For example, the Holy Spirit is actually involved in our response to God – even before we say 'Yes!' to God, the Holy Spirit has been at work within us, prompting us to make this response. There is, of course, a long-standing debate within Christianity upon the nature and extent of the role of the Holy Spirit in conversion, which it is impossible to go into at this point. It is not, however, a debate which need trouble you as you try to explain Christianity to your friends!

7

God

Inevitably, you are going to want to talk about God to your friends. And here you may encounter a cluster of objections which it is helpful to be able to meet. There are four main areas of difficulty, which we'll explore individually.

God doesn't exist anyway

You will very often find yourself immediately confronted with an objection which goes something like this: 'Maybe it was easy for people to believe in God one or thousand years ago – but nowadays it's impossible. God's existence has been disproved.' In fact, this is just not the case. Yet God's existence can neither be conclusively proved nor disproved. In the end, both the atheist and the Christian take their positions as a matter of faith. The famous comment of the Russian writer Boris Pasternak, author of *Dr Zhivago*, is worth noting here: 'I am an atheist who has lost his faith.'

This point is important, as most atheists and agnostics will probably be prepared to admit the *possibility* (however slight!) of God's existence. Their difficulty often lies in accepting that the existence of God is actually relevant to them. God's existence cannot be *disproved* conclusively, as we shall show in what follows. Once the possibility of God's existence is conceded, the argument will take a very different direction. You can then begin to explain some of the reasons why Christians believe in God – for example, by asking what happened at the resurrection, and what its implications are (see chapter 5). The further reading suggested at the end of the book will be helpful in this connection.

Nevertheless, you are likely to encounter people who feel that God's existence can indeed be disproved. We shall look at the two most common arguments against the existence of God which you are likely to encounter.

God is just some kind of wish-fulfilment

This theory has an interesting intellectual pedigree, going back to the Hegelian writer Ludwig Feuerbach in the 1830s, and being developed by Sigmund Freud in the early twentieth century. The argument goes something like this. Human beings basically want God to exist. Now, as Voltaire once said, 'If God didn't exist, it would be necessary to invent him.' And what Christians have done is to invent God. The human longing for the existence of God is projected on to an imaginary heavenly screen. God is a sort of wish-fulfilment: he isn't really there, but Christians imagine that he is because they want him to be there. You have probably heard this sort of idea being discussed already. There are three main responses which you can make.

1. This is not a proof that God doesn't exist – it's simply an assertion that he doesn't. It's a hypothesis, a theory, and certainly not an established fact! Sigmund Freud's explanation of religious belief, for example, is still regarded by some people as having discredited Christianity – yet it is evident that Freud's allegedly 'scientific' approach to Christianity is hopelessly influenced by outdated nineteenth-century rationalist presup-

positions. The issue has been prejudged, not scientifically studied.

2. It appears to rest upon a rather basic logical mistake. The argument seems to go like this:

Premise 1. The fact that we want something to exist doesn't mean that it does exist.

Premise 2.   We want God to exist.

Conclusion.   Therefore God does not exist.

But the conclusion doesn't follow from the premises! Let's suppose that you want a large milk shake after a really tedious lecture. Obviously, the fact that you want one doesn't mean that one will exist for that very reason! On the other hand, it doesn't mean that one cannot exist, just because you happen to want it! Whether you want something or not actually has no direct bearing on whether it exists or not.

Anyway, you could develop this argument in a most uncomfortable manner.

Premise 1. The fact that we do not want something to exist does not mean that it does not exist.

Premise 2. Atheists do not want God to exist.

Conclusion: Therefore God does exist.

The same basic logical error is still being made – but this time the boot is on the other foot! This time it is atheism, it is being suggested, which is indulging in 'wish-fulfilment'.

Atheists do not want God to exist – and therefore they invent his non-existence to support their wishes! The 'wishful thinking' argument can cut both ways. It is not particularly difficult to think of people who have very good reasons for hoping that God doesn't exist – for example, the commandant of a Nazi extermination camp, who is hardly likely to view his future judgment with much enthusiasm. For such a person, belief in the non-existence of God is unquestionably wishful thinking. So

108

does it follow that God *does* exist for this reason? Certainly not!

C. S. Lewis, however, suggested that the fact that many people feel some deep desire for God, which no physical thing could ever satisfy, actually did point to the existence of God. Lewis pointed out that human feelings of need (like hunger and thirst) pointed to the means by which they could be satisfied (by food and drink). Why, he asked, should not the same thing be true of our spiritual hunger and thirst? Did not they point to the means by which they could be satisfied? Lewis' famous sermon 'The Weight of Glory' (originally published in 1949) develops this point with great force, and would be particularly interesting to anyone studying in the field of literature.

3. You could point out that this alleged 'disproof' of God's existence seems to work on the assumption that the existence of God guarantees you some sort of easy ride through life. God is seen as some sort of spiritual consolation, who makes life more bearable for you. Now it is certainly true that a relationship with God does alter our entire outlook on life.

But what about the martyrs, you might ask? What about those who felt that God was asking them to give up their lives for his sake, or asking them to do things which were most uncomfortable? The first Christians often ended up getting martyred for their faith – and if that faith was just some sort of consoling thought to help them cope with life, it's very difficult to see why they should have ended up suffering and giving their lives in the name of 'consolation'! Perhaps there is a danger that some sort of 'wish-fulfilment' might underlie faith, at least for some Christians – but the suggestion that it underlies the faith of *all*, or even *most*, Christians is not to be taken too seriously.

In the end, the idea of God as a 'wish-fulfilment' is an interesting hypothesis, lacking any experimental foundation or proof, which seems to rest upon a basic logical error. Christians can hardly be expected to give up their faith in God on the basis of such a flimsy argument.

The Marxist critique of Christianity

Despite the world-wide collapse of Marxism, this continues to be one of the more influential criticisms of Christian faith you are likely to come across in student circles. In view of this, we shall spend some time dealing with it. Curiously, however, most students seem remarkably ignorant of what Marx actually said. You may well find that your friends who argue that Marx has 'disproved' Christianity have the most superficial acquaintance with what Marx actually said. In fact, Marx's criticism of Christianity has no bearing on whether God exists or not – or, indeed, upon *any* major Christian doctrine. Let's examine this criticism.

Marx argues that religion (and he makes no attempt to distinguish the various religions) comes about through the human social and economic situation. Religion arises from a specific social and economic situation, and in turn supports that situation. For Marx, any social and economic system which is basically capitalist will inevitably produce religion as a means of comforting those who are oppressed (thus diverting their attention from revolution) and justifying the position of those who rule. Religion is 'the opium of the people', consoling the workers in their unjust situation, and also diverting their attention from the present world. Religion prevents social change.

Marx then develops these ideas further. If the social and economic situation can be changed, there will no longer be any need for religion. Religion is basically the result of unjust social conditions: when the revolution comes, these conditions will be overthrown, and religion will simply disappear of its own accord. Marx's theory of the 'historical inevitability of socialism' (no longer, incidentally, regarded as correct by most social scientists) points to Christianity and all other religions fading away as socialism gradually gains the upper hand. There will no longer be any need for it. The communist revolution will eliminate the causes of religion, and thus it will simply disappear. Let's use Marx's own terms: religion is a symptom of socio-economic alienation within capitalism – so that if you remove this alienation through the communist revolution, religion will become superfluous.

We are now in a position to begin responding to this criticism of Christianity. The most important response concerns the way in which Marx handles Christianity.

Marx never seems to make the slightest attempt to deal with the truth-claims of Christianity. For Marx, religion is wrong (because it delays the revolution and supports the ruling classes): as Christianity is a religion, it is wrong for that very reason. This, however, is a distressingly inadequate analysis of Christianity. Marx's materialism leads him to dismiss any concept of a spiritual realm, including the existence and relevance of God. 'Religion' is just a social phenomenon, having no contacts with a reality lying beyond the material world. Marx seems to feel that you can dismiss the truth of a religion because that religion gets in the way of his vision of a communist society. Where is there any indication that Marx has shown that a basic Christian belief – for example, the resurrection – is *wrong?* The only substantial criticism which Marx can level at Christianity is that it gets in the way of his vision of a socialist society. It is inconvenient, perhaps – but it remains to be shown that it is wrong.

This point is of central importance in responding to the Marxist critique of Christianity. However, certain other points might be made. For example, Marx seems to base some of his criticism of Christianity upon his experience of the social and political role of some of the Christian churches in nineteenth-century Europe. Marx correctly noted that these churches tended to support the status quo, and generally lent their support to the ruling classes of their day.

Marx seems to have drawn from this observation the conclusion that Christianity universally supports oppression. Marx's criticism of 'Christianity' is important, in that it demonstrates how easy it is for Christian churches to become too closely linked with the establishment – but it is not a fundamental criticism of Christianity itself. It is not an essential feature of the Christian faith that it *should* be linked with the social establishment.

Marx may legitimately challenge the Christian church at this point, reminding it of its need to foster just social conditions. Furthermore, the Christian church should listen to his criticisms, and attempt to respond to them. His criticisms apply to the Christian church, however, rather than to Christianity – in other words, to Christian institutions rather than the Christian faith. They apply primarily to the way in which Christianity is applied. Marx persistently seems to think that Christianity can be identified with the medieval papacy or the Protestant church-state establishment of the nineteenth century. He criticizes the manner in which Christianity is applied, rather than Christianity itself. But he has not gone even the slightest way towards 'disproving' any Christian doctrine, let alone the existence of God.

Another point may be made here against the Marxist analysis of religion. There is a very obvious and serious contradiction between experience and theory here. Religion should, according to Marx, have died away in communist societies. In fact, there is no evidence that this has happened. In an effort to make theory and reality come together, certain communist societies attempted to suppress Christianity by force: this, however, has now been generally recognized as having been totally counter-productive. It also seems to suggest a certain lack of faith among Marxists in their analysis of the causes of religion: why the need to forcibly suppress something which should naturally fade away? Marx's analysis of the causes of religion would certainly seem to require revision.

Although Marxism now gives every indication of being in a state of permanent decline on university campuses throughout the world, it still represents an important way of understanding the world which still attracts some students, particularly in the developing regions of the world. It is for this reason that it is important to understand its basic ideas. One of the most penetrating studies of Marx's critique of Christianity is by the highly respected German writer Hans Küng. In his helpful work *Does God exist?*, Küng concludes:

> Marx never seriously came to terms with the biblical understanding of God and man and with the message of Jesus Christ and consequently was not at all familiar with the 'social principles of Christianity' (he was even inclined to think that the first Christian communities practised cannibalism when they met for the eucharist). Hence, in his presentation, Christianity appears as a power ideology, determined purely by economic and social interests, with a church subordinated to the state, justifying all injustice in the here and now with an illusory promise of happiness in the hereafter. What is properly and specifically Christian remained alien to Marx throughout his life.

Your responsibility is to ensure that modern student Marxists are presented with a reliable version of 'what is properly and specifically Christian', and that students influenced by the Marxist critique of Christianity are made aware of its weaknesses.

How can I believe in God when there is such suffering and pain in the world?

For many people, suffering is an obstacle to faith. 'How can I believe in God,' they ask, 'when I see so much suffering in the world?' This question tends to be asked for two very different reasons. First, your friend may find this an intellectual difficulty. Secondly, your friend may have seen a relative suffer, or experienced considerable suffering, and thus find it an emotional difficulty as well. It is helpful to work out which of these two situations your friend is in, as it may affect what you say to them.

Let's begin by outlining some points you could make to someone who finds suffering an intellectual difficulty.

1. The existence of pain and suffering was not thought to be a reason for not believing in God until the seventeenth century. The respected philosopher Alasdair MacIntyre (once a Marxist-inclined atheist, now a Christian) argues persuasively in his famous work *The Religious Significance of Atheism* that 'the God in whom the nineteenth and twentieth centuries came to disbelieve had been invented only in the seventeenth century.' People knew all about pain and suffering before then – but they didn't regard them as calling God's existence into question! Only recently (since the Enlightenment) have they been seen as doing this.

So what has changed? The facts – or the way we look at them? The facts are much the same as they always have been – but it is only recently that the existence of pain and suffering have been seen as calling God's existence into question. Might this difficulty not be due simply to a change in intellectual fashions?

2. Is there any reason for supposing that God could have created a world in which there were no pain and suffering? David Hume, the great Scottish philosopher, pointed out that we couldn't claim that the world we know is 'the best of all possible worlds', as we didn't have any other worlds to compare it with! Yet for the same reason, we can't say that there could be a *better* world. We may well feel that this world could have been put together in a different way, thus avoiding suffering and pain – but in the end we just can't prove this.

3. We can't blame God for all suffering and pain. As C. S. Lewis remarks, 'It is men, not God, who have produced racks, whips, prisons, slavery, guns, bayonets and bombs.' Equally, it is largely through human greed that poverty and starvation arise. As relief agencies emphasize, there is more than enough food in the world to prevent starvation: the problem arises through the greed of those who have more than enough.

4. Suffering is not just a difficulty for Christianity! There is no religious or philosophical system, except one, which can explain the problems of suffering and evil. The exception is 'dualism', which sees a permanent conflict between the forces of good and evil. Dualism has no difficulty with suffering or evil: they arise through the great battle that is going on between the good and the evil gods, as they wrestle for control of the world. Pain and suffering are caused by the actions of the evil god. This neatly explains the problem of suffering and evil – but at what a high price! The idea of 'dualism' brings with it a whole range of new problems, as C. S. Lewis so persuasively demonstrated in *Mere Christianity*! But are we to dismiss all these great religious and philosophical systems, simply because of one difficulty that they all share?

For those who find suffering more of an emotional difficulty, the following points may be helpful.

1. Suffering and pain are a problem particularly because they seem to call God's goodness into question. They suggest that he may not be the good and loving God who we thought he was. Yet against this, we have to set God's total commitment to our well-being and ultimate salvation which we can see in the cross. 'God so loved the world that he gave his only Son' (John 3:16). The Son of God himself suffered and died for us. Is it conceivable that the God who loved us so much should turn against us? Martin Luther, the great German Reformer, felt that the only way of dealing with the problem of pain and suffering was to think about Christ dying upon the cross. In his pain and suffering we see the Son of God working out our salvation. He went through that pain and suffering for us.

A quotation from a former Archbishop of Canterbury, William Temple, makes these points very well. '"There cannot be a God of love," men say, "because if there was, and he looked down upon the world, his heart would break." The church points to the cross and says, "It did break." "It is God who made the world," men say. "It is he who should bear the load." The church points to the cross, and says, "He did bear it."'

2. It cannot be emphasized too strongly that God does not will suffering upon us. Let's explore this point. Creation involves risk. Imagine two parents, lovingly bringing a child into the world. He means everything to them, and they love him dearly. They do everything that they can for him. They explain to him about good and evil. Then the child grows up, and rebels against his parents. He becomes addicted to cocaine, and in his desperate search for enough of the drug to meet his addiction, he ends up robbing and killing. Were the

116

parents responsible? In one sense, yes – after all, they brought the child into this world. Yet in another, they are obviously not – they did all they could to guide him into the right course of life. They loved him, and did all that they could for him. Even now – with their son branded a narcotics addict, a robber and a killer – they still love him. They would do anything to help him, and restore him.

Can you see the parallels between God and those parents? God doesn't want us to suffer. He does everything he can to keep us from suffering, or inflicting suffering upon others. He tells us what is right and what is wrong, in order that suffering may be eliminated or kept to a minimum. Yet the freedom he gave us can be used for good or for evil. And, as history and experience sadly confirm, that freedom has been abused. Yet God still loves humanity, and is prepared to do anything he can to help them, and restore them to the way he wished. The death of Christ on the cross underscores this point. The pain and suffering of Christ on the cross show us the suffering and pain which human sin causes God, and invite us to return to him and his ways.

3. Pain and suffering gently bring home to us the fact that we are mortal, and must die. In the last chapter, we noted how humans cannot really bear the thought of death. It is something which they would much prefer to ignore. Suffering and pain are part of a larger picture – the fact that we are mortal and frail humans, who will have to die. We come to see the full importance of the suffering and resurrection of Jesus. As St Paul emphasizes, resurrection comes through death and suffering: it is by sharing Christ's sufferings and death that we will share in his glorious resurrection (Romans 8:15–18).

4. God knows what it is like to suffer. As we saw in an earlier chapter, the doctrine of the incarnation brings home to us that God knows at first hand what it is like to

suffer pain. God doesn't stand aloof from our suffering, but has been through it himself. He knows what it is like. We can turn to God in prayer about suffering, knowing that he understands what it is like.

5. Suffering is a mystery, which we shall never fully understand. Martin Luther compares the life of faith to walking in the dark, not being fully able to see the landscape around us. Many things seem strange and unrelated, simply because we cannot see them properly. When the sun rises, of course, we are enabled to see things clearly, and realize the way they relate to each other. Suffering is like something we encounter while walking in the dark. We feel that it ought not to be there, and cannot understand how it came to be there. But we cannot see the whole picture. In the end, Christians believe that they one day will understand the mystery of suffering. One day, its place and purpose in God's loving plan of salvation will become clear. But on that day, we shall be with the Lord, when suffering itself has passed away (Revelation 21:1–4).

The idea of a personal God is ridiculous

Some of your friends may argue that the idea of a 'personal God' is ridiculous. It's far too unsophisticated for them! When you talk about a 'personal' God, they probably conjure up a mental image of an old man with a long beard dressed up in white, sitting on a cloud somewhere unspecified. 'How can you expect us to believe in a God like that?' they ask. 'It's far too simple!'

An obvious reply is that Christians just *don't* think about God in this way! Newspaper cartoonists certainly do – but the truth of Christianity doesn't depend upon what newspaper cartoonists think God is like! Thinking about God as a person certainly doesn't mean thinking about God as an old man on a cloud. So the first point you could make in response is to criticize this lousy way of thinking about God. However, let's make some more sophisticated points in addition.

The idea of an old man up in the sky would just be one way (and not a very good way, and not a particularly *Christian* way!) of visualizing God. In other words, we need some sort of mental picture to help us think about God. But this mental picture isn't the same as the *reality* of God! I could draw a fairly lousy picture of the President of the United States. You might look at the picture and tell me that it's a lousy picture of the President of the United States – and you'd be right! But what you couldn't argue is that the President of the United States didn't exist, just because I had drawn a bad picture of him.

Nor could you conclude that my picture wasn't a representation of the president – it was just a representation that wasn't good enough to do full justice to him. Now the Christian will argue that no representation of God can ever do justice to him. We need simple representations, or mental pictures, of God if we're going to think about him. Christians, of course, would much prefer to use illustrations taken from Scripture – for example, God as a king, as a father, or as a shepherd (rather than an old man on a cloud). Let's look at the mental picture of God as a shepherd (to use a more scriptural way of thinking about God than an old man on a cloud). We might say that God *is like* a shepherd. But this doesn't mean that God *is* a shepherd! Let's take this point a little further.

In the natural sciences, models are used to help visualize complex systems. For example, the 'kinetic theory of gases' suggests that we think about gas molecules as if they were billiard balls bumping into each other. If we do this, we discover that we can predict some of the properties of gases – for example, the pressure increases when the volume decreases. Now nobody is saying that gas molecules *are* billiard balls! For a start they're much smaller. We're just saying that, in some respects, they *are like* billiard balls. Billiard balls are a useful mental picture of gas molecules, and help us understand the way they behave. In short: they are models of gas molecules.

Now when we talk about God as a person, we aren't saying that God is a human being! What we are saying is that human personal relationships help us understand the way in which God behaves. To put this more formally: human relationships model God. Have you noticed how often Scripture uses human relationships to talk about God? Think of the parable of the wasteful son (see pp. 90–91). Think of how often the Bible talks about God loving us (John 3:16). Think of how often it emphasizes God's faithfulness. Think of how often it talks about God forgiving us, or our need to be reconciled to him. These ideas are drawn from human personal relationships. Just as billiard balls help us visualize and understand gas molecules, so these human personal relationships help us visualize and understand God.

So when we talk about God as a person, we are affirming a whole series of central biblical insights. We aren't saying that God is another human being. We are saying that Christians understand God to behave in ways which are paralleled in the best human relationships. It means discarding inadequate ideas about God – like God as an abstract idea – and affirming the biblical witness to God as one who loves us, meets us, and enters into a relationship with us. Prayer, after all, is basically like talking to another person (notice how Jesus makes this point: Matthew 7:9–11). Christians have to do justice to the way in which God reveals himself in Scripture, and the way in which Christians have experienced him down the ages. And the idea of a 'personal God' and of our relation with him as a 'personal relationship' is a very helpful and proper way of talking and thinking about the 'God and Father of our Lord Jesus Christ' (1 Peter 1:3).

Christians believe in a male God, who has no relevance for women

Earlier, we noted how Scripture used models to help us think about God. These models of God are firmly located in real life. Just as Jesus used real-life parables to make theological points, so the writers of Scripture use models drawn from the experiential world of ancient Palestine to allow us insights into the nature and purposes of God. In that this society was male-dominated, many of these models are male. For example, the idea of the authority of God can only be represented using male imagery – for example, that of a father, a judge or a king. Nevertheless, other models are used. God is often compared to a (genderless) rock, for example, conveying the idea of strength, stability and permanence. Feminine imagery abounds to describe God's care and compassion for his people, which is often likened to the love of a mother for her children. Yet it is not the imagery, but what is being said about God, that is of fundamental importance.

Scripture affirms that kings, shepherds and fathers in ancient Israel society are appropriate models for God. But this use of male models does not mean that God is male, any more than the use of genderless models (such as a rock) means that God is impersonal, or the use of female models (such as mother) imply that God is female. To speak of God as father is to say that the role of the father in ancient Israel allows us insights into the nature of God. It is not to say that God *is* a male human being! Neither male nor female sexuality is to be attributed to God. Sexuality is an attribute of the created order, which cannot be assumed to correspond directly to any such polarity within the Godhead.

The Old Testament avoids attributing sexual functions to God, on account of the strongly pagan overtones of such associations. The Canaanite fertility cults emphasized the sexual functions of both gods and goddesses; the Old Testament refuses to endorse the idea that the gender or the sexuality of God is a significant matter. There is no need to revert to pagan ideas of gods and goddesses to recover the idea that God is neither masculine or feminine; those ideas are already firmly embedded in Scripture. The appeal to an allegedly 'male' God in support of the oppression of women is thus without foundation in the Christian gospel.

We shall explore issues relating to the gospel and women in the concluding chapter of this study. Our attention now turns to a series of difficulties which are raised by trends in Western culture, which are felt especially keenly on university campuses.

Part 3

The Gospel and Modern Culture

8

Cultural pressures and the gospel

It is impossible to be a student on many modern European, North American and Australian university campuses without being aware of the cultural pressures which are working against Christianity. The rise of postmodernism, scepticism, pluralism and relativism have all placed new strains on the witness of students on campus. In this chapter, we shall examine these pressures, and offer some useful responses.

There's no such thing as truth

Christians claim, with the best of authority, to be telling the truth. They are convinced, with excellent reasons, that Christianity:

1. is grounded in the bedrock of history;
2. has a coherent view of reality;
3. is open to, and can make sense of, the data of experience;
4. can hold its own against any other world-view.

So it can be very unsettling when the claim to be telling the truth is met with the response that there is no truth to tell!

One of the most interesting aspects of modern intellectual culture is that it is radically relativist and sceptical. (At least, it is at the moment: intellectual fashions change so quickly and unpredictably that you can never be too sure about these things!) Attitudes such as 'It may be true for you but not true for me' are widepread on many campuses. The three main beliefs of this 'postmodernist' outlook are the following:

1. the relativism of all truth claims;
2. the subjectivity of beliefs and moral convictions;
3. the necessity of pluralism.

Truth is thus often seen as something personal, individual and existential. The idea of truth as something public and universal, which is open to critical examination, has been abandoned by many.

Now that is bad news, in some ways. But it is also good news in others. It means, for example, that Christians no longer have to put up with the patronizing dismissal of their views by those who dismiss them as 'irrational'. This dismissal rests on the assumption that there is some universal 'rationality', by whose standards the gospel fails. Yet that idea, which is typical of the Enlightenment, died out sometime in the last generation (though some folk haven't realized it yet!). Christians can now expect their views to be treated just as seriously as everyone else's, without having them dismissed in this arrogant manner.

This slide into scepticism and relativism is also, however, an irritation to Christians, who want to emphasize the credentials of the gospel. So how can something be done? There are two strategies which work well in these situations, which we shall explore in what follows.

Emphasize the attraction of the gospel

Christianity is both true and attractive. In the past, the strategy adopted in apologetics was to get folk to accept that the gospel was right, and then explain how attractive it was. In a cultural situation which valued truth above all things, this approach made a lot of sense. But the culture has changed, and leaves this approach stranded. In a culture which has little interest in truth, we must begin by bringing out as clearly as possible the attraction of the gospel.

Does this mean abandoning or sidelining the truth of the gospel? Certainly not. The truth of the gospel remains of foundational importance, and must never be compromised. The issue has to do with presentation rather than substance. This means that in apologetic and evangelistic situations we don't give the truth of the gospel the high profile that we once would have. Instead, we put the emphasis on the attractiveness of the gospel, and its power to transform lives. Yet we do this in the full knowledge that what we are saying is *true*. In no way are we losing sight of the truth of the gospel. All that we are doing is acknowledging that, for the moment, nobody wants to hear about truth. If we want to gain a hearing for the gospel in this situation, we must draw on another of the many strengths of the gospel.

For there is another feature of the 'postmodernist' mind which we have not yet noted. This is its renewed interest in religious questions, such as the destiny of humanity after death, the meaning of personhood, and a realization of the spiritual poverty of a purely material approach to life. Despite the difficulties which postmodernism causes, its outlook opens some very exciting possibilities for Christians to explain their faith and its relevance to issues concerning the afterlife, personhood and spirituality.

So take time to explain the difference that the gospel has made to your life. Point out how it has transformed the lives of many on campus, and that it has the power to do so for those around you, in the full knowledge that what you are saying is true. It is no invention, fabrication or fraud, but something grounded in the truth of God himself.

Point out the weakness of relativism
The strategy just explained gets round the cultural aversion to truth by majoring on the very great appeal of the gospel. But there is another approach which confronts this aversion directly. This is to expose the total inadequacy and unacceptability of the relativist position. In some ways, this is a high-risk strategy, as it may offend those you are talking to. However, if it is handled sensitively, it may well open up important inroads for the gospel.

The fundamental belief of relativism is that there is no truth. All views are relative and equally valid. Thus the view that there is no God is just as valid as the view that there is a God. But asking some hard questions will begin to expose the superficiality of this position. For example, the declaration that 'there is no universal truth' is itself a universal statement. This amounts to accepting the truth of universal statements at one moment, only to deny it the next! It has about as much credibility as the Cretan who declares that all Cretans are liars.

Try asking this question: 'Is the view that the earth rotates round the sun as equally valid as the view that the sun rotates round the earth?' Both these views are held today, the former in a Western scientific culture (present on all university campuses), and the latter in primitive cultures who have not been exposed to Western science. It is therefore not a hypothetical question; both views are in existence today. If the relativist declares that both views are equally valid, he or she will have implied that the natural sciences are a complete waste of time. There is no need to bother with scientific investigation, as all views are equally valid. The whole point of natural science is to eliminate options by rigorous investigation, which undermines the relativist position. This kind of argument will be invaluable in dealing with relativists who are studying the sciences, or are familiar with their methods.

Other approaches can be adopted for those studying the liberal arts. For example, try asking this question: 'Was Hitler right in his belief that Jews should be gassed and cremated?' This question puts the relativist in something of a difficulty. If he says that Hitler was not right, he is conceding that not all views are equally valid. By doing this, he has opened the door to a discussion on what is right and wrong, and abandoned any meaningful commitment to relativism. If he tells you that Hitler's view was valid (even if only for himself), he has implicitly endorsed anti-semitic views which would be regarded as totally unacceptable on any modern campus. In addition, he will have supported opinions which are an outrage to any sane system of morality.

Or try asking this question: 'Are Hindus right to demand that widows should be burned alive on their husband's funeral pyres?' Once more, the relativist is in an impossible situation. If she says that they are not right, she will have conceded that there are issues of right and wrong at stake, and thus concede the failure of relativism. On the other hand, if she suggests that it is legitimate for women to be burned alive (forcibly if necessary!), she will find herself the subject of rightful scorn and contempt, by consenting to a position which is clearly deeply offensive to women and to any sane morality.

Relativism is flawed! There is no need to give up on the fundamental Christian insistence that the gospel is as true as it is relevant. It is up to you to judge how best to get round the relativism of your friends, and gain a hearing for the truth and joy of the gospel.

Christians are arrogant in their claims

There can be no doubt that many Christians state and defend their beliefs in highly dogmatic and unthinking ways which alienate their peers, and persuade them that Christianity is only for unthinking arrogant fools. This sort of person is one of the worst possible advertisements for Christianity, and ought to be persuaded to undergo an intense course in personal relations skills as a matter of urgency! But it need not be like this.

You must explain that Christians do not hold their views, or attempt to share them, as a matter of arrogance. They hold them because they believe that they have found something which makes sense and is deeply attractive, and for which they are profoundly grateful. In fact, they are so grateful that they want to share it with everyone else! Why keep a good thing to yourself? Even the most humble person who discovers something wonderful runs the risk of sounding arrogant when they talk about it.

Is a microbiologist being arrogant when he or she declares that penicillin cures blood poisoning? Certainly not! He or she is simply reporting with confidence and pleasure the fact that, after much hard experimental investigation, a cure to blood poisoning has been found and made available. This is good news! And it is the kind of news that is going to change people's lives.

So try not to seem arrogant when you talk about your faith. It's a negative for many people. Don't allow your personality to become a barrier to the gospel. Instead, learn to speak with a quiet and humble confidence about the joy of the gospel, and your hope that others would discover the same joy that you have come to know.

Christianity and other religions

One of the most important issues relating to modern culture concerns other religions. The vast migrations of people from the Indian subcontinent, the Middle East and south-east Asia to Western cities has led to the presence of large communities of non-Christian religions in these cities, and hence at local universities. The theme of 'other religions' is thus likely to be important to Christian students on campus. In what follows, we shall explore some of the issues which arise.

But remember that many students from non-Christian backgrounds will be deeply attracted to the Christian faith, will become Christians, and will eventually return to their own regions of the world as missionaries or pastors. The presence of these students on Western campuses is to be seen as an opportunity, not a problem.

You've got to respect non-Christian religions

You certainly do need to respect non-Christian religions! But that doesn't mean you've got to agree with them, or that they're right. You can treat another person's views with respect as you discuss them with them. And surely the greatest respect that you can show for the religious views of another person is that they are worth discussing?

The appeal to 'respect' usually means 'Back off! Leave things alone!' But the implications of this objection are incredible. It suggests that some religions are so riddled with contradictions and flaws that talking about them will immediately expose them, and cause that person to abandon their faith in favour of Christianity. Any world-view which refuses to engage with another raises the most serious of doubts concerning its credentials.

All religions lead to God

The argument that 'all religions lead to God' is often encountered. The following points will be found helpful. How can all religions lead to God, when some of them have no idea of God at all? This argument rests on the common fallacy that all religions are theistic, which is clearly not the case.

Following the failure of this line of argument, another approach may be used. You may be told that the religions of the world are like different paths leading up the same mountain. They all get to the top, even if they take different routes. This analogy is fatally flawed. It assumes that there is only one peak to the mountain. Yet the religions have very different ideas about what that 'peak' looks like, some being atheist, some monotheist, and some polytheist. A better analogy is that of a mountain with lots of different peaks. The question then becomes: How do I get to the peak I want to? Which is the best peak to reach?

This analogy has, in any case, been chosen by pluralist writers in order to predetermine the conclusion, and it is invalid for this reason. A more Christian analogy would be that of a maze. There are many paths, but only one gets you out!

In this chapter, we have explored some of the issues which arise from modern culture. But there is one of especial importance, which merits an entire chapter to itself. This is the issue of whether Christianity oppresses women, to which we now turn.

9

Does Christianity oppress women?

In recent years, gender-related issues have come to the fore on university campuses. Slogans such as 'religion oppresses women' have become commonplace. Many anti-Christian writers have declared that Christanity is an irrelevance to women. After all, they argue, it believes in a male God and a male redeemer, to note two common criticisms already dealt with (see pp. 59–61; 121–122).

Many Christian students find themselves at a loss to know how to respond to such criticisms. This final chapter of the book will show that while it is true that in the past the Christian church, in common with virtually all of Western society, treated women with less than their full due, this is not an integral element of the Christian gospel. Indeed, as will become clear, the ministry of Jesus Christ was profoundly liberating for women. In view of the complexity and importance of these issues, they will be treated in more depth than other issues in this book, in order to bring out the points of particular importance.

The background to the rise of Christianity
Christianity broke into the settled world of the first century like a tidal wave. It generated a set of new social attitudes and outlooks, all of which it ultimately grounded

in its understanding of the experience of redemption in Jesus Christ. The 'good news' of Jesus Christ was that, through his death and resurrection, a new way of life was made possible for men and women. This new life had many aspects – for example, a new relationship with God, the experience of the presence and power of the risen Christ and of the Holy Spirit. But it also brought into being Christian communities, who shaped their personal and social attitudes and outlooks in line with this new way of life made possible through Jesus Christ.

The world into which Christianity expanded can be thought of as dominated by a mixture of cultures: Jewish, Roman and Greek. Although there was considerable variation within and across these cultures, the general position of women was inferior to men. They were subject to restrictions which had no direct male counterparts. Greek women played an important role in the religious cults of the period. They served in the cults of goddesses, they were allowed to act as prophetesses and visionaries, and were able to participate in most religious rites. But within the household, the wife appears to have been treated primarily as the bearer of children. In Macedonia and Asia Minor, however, women appear to have played a significant role in public life, especially in commerce and politics. In their study of Hellenistic civilization, W. W. Tarn and G. T. Griffith summarize the available historical evidence as follows:

> If Macedonia produced perhaps the most competent group of men the world has yet seen, the women were in all respects the men's counterparts. They played a large part in affairs, received envoys, and obtained concessions from them for their husbands, built temples, founded cities, engaged mercenaries, commanded armies,

held fortresses, and acted on occasions as regents or even co-rulers.

A similar situation existed in Asia Minor and many of the islands of the eastern Aegean, where women featured prominently in both the secular and religious life of the period, even holding public office.

However, it is in Rome that women had the greatest freedom and status. Our historical evidence relates primarily to patrician matrons. While a long-standing tradition laid down that a woman's place of activity was primarily within the home, this did not lead to her being isolated from public life. Indeed, the evidence suggests that Roman patrician women were among the most highly educated members of society. They were more self-confident, more influential and more respected than their counterparts anywhere else in the Mediterranean world of the period.

This was not always the case. At the time of the Roman republic, Roman women appear to have been treated in a manner which parallels that of rabbinic Judaism. For example, a Roman father had the right to kill children he did not want, especially if the child was female, just as he had the power of life or death over his wife. His authority also extended to making marriage arrangements for his daughters. By the end of the Republic, however, these powers had virtually ceased to be binding. Women were increasingly free to make their own marriage arrangements, and take control of their own affairs. Nevertheless, restrictions remained. Even at the time of the Roman empire, women were prohibited from holding public office.

All this contrasted sharply with the much more restricted role placed upon women in both public and religious life in Israel at the time of Christ. It is clear that women in Rome, Asia Minor, Macedonia and the Aegean islands were far more liberated than those of rural Judea, or even urban Jerusalem, at the time of Christ. The relevance of all this to our theme will be obvious. Christianity had its origins in a deeply patriarchal society, where the social role of women was severely restricted by rabbinic Judaism. Yet Christianity expanded into regions in which women were more highly esteemed, and in which they had a much higher profile.

This seems to have had a major consequence. In regions such as Asia Minor and Macedonia, in which Judaism had only a slight influence, the emerging Christian churches were able to give women a status which would have been unthinkable in a Jewish context. The missionary aims of the early church were to convert both Jews and Gentiles. In the home territory of Judaism, this meant that Christianity was obliged to respect at least some of the social conventions of Judaism; but in Asia Minor and Europe, it was free from such constraints.

Incidents in the Acts of the Apostles are of importance in this respect. For example, in Acts 16, we read of Lydia, clearly a well-connected and important business woman who had assumed a significant role in the local Christian community at Philippi. Lydia and her household were the first converts in Macedonia, and her house appears to have become both a staging post for missionaries in the region, and the centre of a Christian church.

> One of those listening was a woman named Lydia, a dealer in purple cloth from the city of Thyatira, who was a worshipper of God. The Lord opened her heart to respond to Paul's message. When she and the members of her household were baptised, she invited us to her home. 'If you consider me a believer in the Lord,'

136

she said, 'come and stay at my house.' And she persuaded us. (Acts 16:14–15)

Luke skilfully brings out how a woman, who had been marginalized by Judaism, became a central figure in the local church, and had the distinction of being the first baptized Christian convert in Europe. It is clear from Paul's letter to the Philippians that women continued to play a major and honoured role in that church. Surveying the evidence relating to the church at Philippi, W. D. Davies remarks that:

> in the earnest and undiscriminating preaching of Paul to the women at the riverside, in the baptism of Lydia, in the influence of Euodias and Syntyche, in the prayers and service of the honoured widows, and in the warmth of the welcome Crescens' sister could expect, we may be glimpsing the new kind of status the Christian church could afford to women, especially in a place where the Jewish presence was not strong.

The New Testament witness: Early Christian attitudes towards women

To understand how liberating Christianity proved to be to women, it is necessary to explore the attitudes to women found in the New Testament. The most obvious place to begin such a study is the ministry of Jesus Christ himself, in which we find a positive attitude towards women unlike anything found the rabbinic Judaism of the period.

Jesus Christ and women

We may begin by exploring the attitude of Jesus himself towards women – attitudes which ought to be a central part of the heritage of the Christian church. Throughout his ministry, Jesus shows himself to be affirming of women in a manner which would have been virtually unthinkable within the dominantly patriarchal outlook of the rabbinical Judaism of the period. The following points are of especial importance.

1. Jesus' commendation of the single state as a legitimate calling for those to whom it was given stands in sharp contrast to traditional Palestinian views of a human duty to marry and procreate. As a result, women who chose to follow Jesus were able to assume roles other than those of wife or mother.

2. Jesus treats women as human subjects, rather than as objects or possessions. Throughout his ministry, Jesus can be seen engaging with and affirming women – often women who were treated as outcasts by contemporary Jewish society on account of their origins (*e.g.* Syro-Phoenicia or Samaria) or their life-style (*e.g.* prostitutes).

3. Jesus refused to make women scapegoats in sexual matters – for example, adultery. The patriarchal assumption that men are corrupted by fallen women is conspicuously absent from his teaching and attitudes, most notably towards prostitutes and the woman taken in adultery. The Talmud's recommendation that its readers (assumed to be men) should 'not converse much with women, as this will eventually lead you to unchastity' is studiously ignored by Jesus, who made a point of talking to women (John 4 being an especially celebrated instance).

4. The traditional view that a woman was 'unclean' during the period of menstruation was dismissed by Jesus, who made it clear that it is only moral impurity which defiles a person (Mark 7:1–23). Women could not be excluded from acts of worship for this traditional reason.

5. Women were an integral part of the group of people who gathered round Jesus, and were affirmed by

him, often to the dismay of the Pharisees and other religious traditionalists. Not only were women witnesses to the crucifixion; they were also the first witnesses to the resurrection. The only Easter event to be explicitly related in detail by all four of the gospel writers is the visit of the women to the tomb of Jesus. Yet Judaism dismissed the value of the testimony or witness of a women, regarding only men as having significant legal status in this respect. The greatest news that the world has ever known was thus first disclosed to women! Interestingly, Mark tells us the names of these women witnesses – Mary Magdalene, Mary the mother of James, and Salome – *three times* (Mark 15:40, 47; 16:1), but never bothers to mention the names of any male disciples who were around at the time. (It might also be worth noting that it was a man who betrayed Jesus, and a group of men who crucified Jesus!)

6. The gospels frequently portray women as being much more spiritually perceptive than men. For example, Mark portrays the male disciples as having little faith (Mark 4:40; 6:52), while commending women – a woman is praised for her faith (Mark 5:25–34), a foreign woman for responding to Jesus (Mark 7:24–30), and a widow is singled out as an example to follow (Mark 12:41–44).

Luke's gospel is of particular interest in relation to Jesus' attitude to women. For example, Luke brings out clearly how women are among the 'oppressed' who are liberated by the coming of Jesus. Luke also sets out his material in a parallel manner, to emphasize that both men and women are involved in and benefit from the ministry of Jesus. For example, the following passages demonstrate this parallelism especially clearly:

Luke 1:11–20, 26–38 Zacharias and Mary
Luke 2:25–38 Simeon and Anna
Luke 7:1–17 a centurion and a widow

Luke 13:18–21   a man with mustard seed and a woman with leaven

Luke 15:4–10   a man with sheep and a woman with coins

By this arrangement of material, Luke expresses the fact that men and women stand together side by side before God. They are equal in honour and grace; they are endowed with the same gifts and have the same responsibilities.

Luke also draws our attention to the significant role of women in the spreading of the gospel. For example, Luke 8:2–3 indicates that 'many women' were involved in early evangelistic endeavours, referring to the Twelve being accompanied by 'some women who had been cured of evil spirits and diseases: Mary (called Magdalene) from whom seven demons had come out; Joanna the wife of Cuza, the manager of Herod's household; Susanna; and many others.' The inclusion of women in such a significant role would have seemed incomprehensible to the male-dominated society of contemporary Palestine.

Women in the Acts of the Apostles

In the Acts of the Apostles, Luke emphasizes the role of providing hospitality for missionaries. As we have already noted, this was of major importance in establishing the church in Europe, with women converts such as Lydia making their homes available as house churches and staging-posts for missionaries. Luke appears to be concerned to bring out clearly the important historical point that the early church attracted significant numbers of prominent women in cultures which gave them a much greater social role than in Judaism, and offered them a significant role in the overall evangelistic and pastoral ministry of the early church.

In particular, Luke singles out Priscilla and Aquila as a husband-and-wife team who were engaged in an evangelistic and teaching ministry (Acts 18:1–3, 24–26), not least in relation to Apollos. Interestingly, the name of the woman precedes that of her husband. As many scholars of antiquity point out, it is unusual for a woman's name to precede that of her husband. Perhaps Priscilla had a higher social rank than her husband, or was more significant in Christian circles. The priority given to Priscilla clearly suggests that Luke regards her as taking priority over Aquila in terms of the teaching ministry exercised by the couple.

Many other examples could be given. Paul commends to the Roman church 'our sister Phoebe, a servant of the church at Cenchrea' (Romans 16:1), commenting on how helpful she had been to him. 1 Timothy 3:11 and 5:9–10 also clearly point to women having a ministerial role, exercising a recognized and authorized ministry of some form within the church.

The New Testament scholar Ben Witherington III summarizes his extensive analysis of the role of women in the early church as follows:

> Why . . . did Luke go to such lengths to stress and indeed support the role of women in the earliest Christian churches? It is a reasonable hypothesis that when Luke wrote in the last quarter of the first century there was still considerable resistance to such ideas among his audience, and so the case had to be made in some detail. Though we have not seen evidence in this chapter to warrant the conclusion that Luke totally rejected the patriarchal framework of his culture, he is exercised, like Paul, to stress a transformed vision of such a framework and to

141

uphold a model of servant leadership (Luke 22:24–30). At the same time, however, Luke stresses the viability of women performing various tasks of ministry for the community. Luke and Paul stand together in maintaining a tension between the reformation of the old order and the affirmation of the new in Christ.

Paul's attitude to women in 1 Corinthians

It is clear that Paul's approach is profoundly liberating, implying new freedoms for women. Spiritual gifts, Paul insists, are not bestowed on the basis of gender, race or class. Whatever gifts God has bestowed must be recognized and put to use. But Paul is clearly aware that this universalization will raise problems in terms of its practical application in matters of church life and within Christian families. His letters therefore include discussion of a number of sensitive areas, which I propose to deal with. Both the passages in question are drawn from Paul's letters to Corinth.

It must be stressed that the Corinthian situation appears to have been especially difficult, with the issue of personal freedom emerging as being of major importance. Paul is obliged to lay down limits to Christian freedom, particularly in relation to spiritual gifts, in order to prevent the church from degenerating into chaos, or hindering the spread of the gospel by scandalizing people for cultural, not theological, reasons.

1 Corinthians 11:2–16

The issue raised by this passage concerns whether women should cover their heads in public worship. The passage in question is notoriously difficult to interpret, largely because we do not know enough about the Corinthian church, or local Corinthian culture, to be sure that we have understood Paul's point. There seems to be no explanation forthcoming from modern scholars as to why Paul regards it as obvious that men should have their heads uncovered, and women their heads covered, at worship. One suggestion has been that a woman with an uncovered head might have been mistaken for a prostitute. In that Corinth was noted as a centre of prostitution, partly on account of the fact that it was a port, it is possible that this explanation would make sense of Paul's recommendation. However, there is not enough evidence to support this contention. Nor is it clear quite why he regards it as obvious that men should cut their hair shorter than women.

The basic point at issue seems to be what is decorous or respectful within the context of the local Corinthian situation – in other words, a local custom which Paul is concerned to uphold, possibly in the belief that this will be more culturally acceptable within the local context. From what we know of the Corinthian Christian community, it is likely that there were converted Jews among their number. Paul may well have been anxious not to scandalize such Jews, and for this reason, requests that what is known to have been a traditional Jewish custom be maintained in this context.

Other interpretations are also possible. In an important article, the Cambridge New Testament scholar Morna Hooker argues that the reference to 'authority' in 1 Corinthians 11:10 does not refer to a man's authority over a woman, but to a woman's authority in her own right to pray within the congregation. It is important to note that Paul does not speak of 'subjection' in this context, but of 'authority'. Hooker argues that Paul here maintains the basic point made so forcefully in Galatians 3:24 – that there is neither male nor female, for all are one in Christ, but that the differences between male and female remain as part of the creation ordering, and must be respected. If Hooker is right, Paul's concern is to stress that Christian women have a new status and authority in Christ, rather than to legislate on headwear.

The issue of length of hair is generally thought to relate to pagan religious beliefs and practices, which Paul would have wished to forbid in his congregation. For example, a number of scholars have pointed out that, within contemporary Corinthian culture, hair style or length was a sign of sexual or religious practices. Long hair for a man could indicate homosexuality, as could short hair on a women. Equally, dishevelled hair on the part of a woman was often linked with the ecstatic mystery cults, such as the frenzied rituals associated with the Isis cult. If this is the case, we are dealing with recommendations from Paul which are grounded in the particularities of the Corinthian situation of the time, and which need not be regarded as binding upon Christians for all time. Paul's recommendations would seem to relate to local Corinthian circumstances, which no longer apply.

1 Corinthians 14:33–35

This passage is also very difficult to interpret. Let me set it out in full, before trying to explore its meaning.

> As in all the congregations of the saints, women should remain silent in the churches. They are not allowed to speak, but must be in submission, as the Law says. If they want to inquire about something, they should ask their own husbands at home; for it is disgraceful for a woman to speak in the church.

Once more, I need to stress that we do not know enough about the Corinthian situation to be sure that we fully understand the context in which this passage is set. However, it seems that the same general considerations which I set out in relation to 1 Corinthians 11:2–16 are relevant here. Paul is concerned to maintain decorum and propriety in the churches, to avoid scandalizing anyone. Mary Hayter summarizes this position as follows:

> In these verses . . . [Paul] was governed by the overriding concern not to violate the rules of propriety that were generally observed at the time. This meant that in volatile situations a woman's personal freedom 'in Christ' might have to be suspended for the sake of the Body of Christ as a whole (compare the principle behind 1 Corinthians 9, where Paul encourages the sacrifice of personal 'rights' to avoid putting obstacles in the way of the spread of the gospel).

The most natural interpretation of these verses is that most women in Corinth would not be well-educated, whereas men generally were. The recommendation that women consult their husbands for explanation is not an assertion of the superiority of male over female, but simply a pragmatic recognition that, in contemporary Corinth, men were better educated and informed than women.

Furthermore, the prevailing cultural norms of both Judaism and Roman society were strongly opposed to women making public pronouncements. While Roman matrons were free to say what they liked at home, there was considerable cultural resistance to their being allowed to speak in public. Corinth was a Roman colony, and it is likely that there were Roman members in the Corinthian church. Paul appears to have been concerned that their sense of what was decorous and culturally acceptable might be outraged if women were to speak in public. Yet there is an additional consideration here. A survey of the various uses of the Hebrew words for silence reveals that the only time silence is associated with submission in the Old Testament is out of respect for God (Habakkuk 2:20), for someone in a position of authority (Judges 3:19), or for wise men noted for their knowledge and counsel (Job 29:21). Job 29:21 implies the silence of respect for a teacher, and has a direct bearing on Paul's advice. Paul's demand for silence is a demand for respect for someone who is recognized as wise and in authority in the church.

A further point of major importance here is Paul's concern for orderliness in public worship. A major concern of Paul over the behaviour of the Corinthian Christians centred on the disorderliness of services – for example, people arriving late for the Lord's Supper:

> When you come together, it is not the Lord's Supper you eat, for as you eat, each of you goes ahead without waiting for anybody else. One remains hungry, another gets drunk. Don't you have homes to eat and drink in? Or do you despise the church of God and humiliate those who have nothing? What shall I say to you? Shall I praise you for this? Certainly not! (1 Corinthians 11:20–22)

Disorder, then, is something to which Paul objects. His advice is intended to avoid chaos in public worship, and ensure a respectful hearing for those with spiritual gifts or words of knowledge.

The place of women in Christian thought

'There is neither Jew nor Greek, slave nor free, male nor female, for you are all one in Christ Jesus' (Galatians 3:28).

This verse stands as the foundation of a Christian approach to differences of gender, class or race. Paul affirms that being 'in Christ' transcends all social, ethnic and sexual barriers. Perhaps this vigorous and unambiguous statement was provoked by the local situation in Galatia, in which Judaizers (that is to say, people who wished Christians to retain the traditions of Judaism) were attempting to retain customs or beliefs which encouraged or justified such distinctions. Paul does not mean that people stop being Jews or Greeks, or male and female, as a result of their conversions. It does mean that these distinctions, while remaining, cease to have any saving significance. They may have importance in the eyes of the world; yet in the sight of God, and within the Christian community, they are transcended by the union between Christ and the believer. Paul's affirmation has two major consequences. First, it declares that there are no barriers of gender, race or social status to the gospel. The gospel is universal in its scope. Secondly, it clearly implies that, while Christian faith does not abolish the particularities of one's existence, they are to be used to glorify God in whatever situation we find ourselves.

Christianity thus laid the foundations for the radical undermining of traditional attitudes towards both women and slaves at two levels:

1. It asserted that all were one in Christ – whether Jew or Gentile, whether male or female, whether master or slave. Differences of race, gender or social position were declared to place no obstacles between all believers sharing the same common relationship with the risen Christ.

2. It insisted that all – whether Jew or Gentile, whether male or female, whether master or slave – could share in the same Christian fellowship, and worship together. Society might force each of these groups to

behave in different manners; but within the Christian community, all were to be regarded as brothers and sisters in Christ.

These developments did not lead to an immediate alteration in existing attitudes towards either women or slaves. Theory always appears to have preceded practice, with the practice being affected by a variety of factors, including the cultural acceptability of the development in question. Nevertheless, it was equivalent to placing a theoretical timebomb under them. It was only a matter of time before the foundations of these traditional distinctions would be eroded to the point at which they could no longer be maintained. As the Roman historian Harold Mattingley once pointed out, 'Christianity made no attempt to abolish slavery at one blow, but it undermined its basis by admitting slaves into the same religious fellowship as their masters.'

The general principle which thus emerges can be stated as follows. The New Testament makes it clear that there is a theoretical equality amongst Christians. Differences of racial origin, gender or class are relativized and abolished by the new relationship with the risen Christ which arises through faith in him. Yet the practical outworking of these developments is seen as a long-term issue. Cultural attitudes modify these radical theoretical beliefs. The theoretical equality of all believers may not be culturally acceptable in certain contexts. As a result, theory may not be able to pass into practice in one cultural context, while it may in another.

On the basis of what has been said, it is clear that the Christian gospel gave a new status to women, as it did to others (such as Gentiles and slaves) who had hitherto been regarded as marginalized within Judaism. However, there was, as we have seen, a genuine tension between these new attitudes and values and the generally patriarchal structure of family and society in the first century. The New Testament is not revolutionary, in the sense that it does not make demands for a radical and violent overthrow of the existing order of things. Rather, it lays the foundations for a new set of attitudes which, if generally accepted, would have transformed society.

But how could the church get those values accepted in a society which was clearly not ready to receive them? To get society to accept Christian values and attitudes, society had first to be made Christian. This meant that evangelism was seen as a priority. Yet evangelism, then as now, had to proceed by ensuring that people outside the church were not unnecessarily scandalized. The acceptance of the gospel itself was prior to the acceptance of the new values which it embodied. As a result, there is a tension between the theological affirmation of the equality of all, and the apologetic recognition of divergence and diversity.

Many scholars have noted how Christianity was treated with contempt by educated Romans and Greeks in its first two centuries. In order to gain any kind of hearing for the good news of the gospel, at least some degree of cultural accommodation was necessary. The early Christians chose not to dilute the gospel message, but attempted to demonstrate the social acceptability of Christianity. Inevitably, this meant bringing Christian attitudes towards women more into line with those which prevailed in the wider community. By the end of the fourth century, such social pressures seem to have led to the neglect, or perhaps even suppression, of the ministerial roles of women within the church. But this is simply a response to historical circumstances. It is not integral to the gospel!

The oppression of women in the past by the church is a matter of history; it is time that Christianity triumphed over the institution of the church at this point. For, as we have stressed, sin is structural, not just personal. The church itself, as much as individual Christians, is prone to sin. It is a reminder of how the past history of the church can become a present argument against Christianity, and an incentive to reform the church of our own day and age, in order that it can bear a more effective witness to our own generation.

In the end, however, it must be stressed that it is not the Christian church which is itself the good news. The church and its members are merely the clay jars in which the great treasure of the gospel is placed. The church is all too often a poor witness to the great joy and freedom which the gospel brings. The good news of Jesus Christ is that men and women, of whatever race or social status, are offered forgiveness and the hope of eternal life through his death and resurrection.

Conclusion

This book has aimed to encourage you, by reassuring you that the Christian faith makes sense, is attractive to outsiders, and can be defended against its modern critics on campus and elsewhere. You don't need to feel defensive about being a Christian any more! In bringing this work to a close, it makes sense to set out three basic points of vital importance to your witness to students on campus, and to others far beyond.

1. Get to know and understand the Christian faith. You will find that your own faith is deepened and strengthened as you appreciate and understand more about what Christians believe. And avoid jargon! Don't assume that the people you are talking to will understand what 'salvation' or 'eternal life' mean. You need to explain such words in plain English – and that means you need to understand them yourself!

The two following books are of especial value in this context:

Bruce Milne, *Know the Truth* (Leicester: Inter-Varsity Press, and Downers Grove: InterVarsity Press, 1982), which focuses on the biblical foundations of Christian faith.

Alister E. McGrath, *Christian Theology: An Introduction* (Oxford/Cambridge, MA: Blackwell, 1994), which is stronger on the historical development of Christian thought, including major sections on the Reformation, modern thought, and so on.

2. Take the trouble to listen to people, and work out where they are coming from and what they are looking for. Don't dismiss their ideas with a scathing 'Well, I can't accept that, because I'm a Christian.' Try to be more engaging: 'That's interesting. Actually, I'm a Christian, and I'd see that in a different way . . .' Try to initiate conversations which will lead to a discussion of Christianity, rather than a confrontational dismissal of their ideas and values. Being dismissive simply suggests to others that you are being shallow and unthinking.

3. Take the trouble to think through how the gospel can be 'good news' for your friends. Avoid being mechanical! You should ask yourself how you can best bring out the full wonder and joy of the gospel for the people you are talking to. Which of its many aspects is the most appropriate for them? And how can it best be explained to them? One of the great joys of evangelism is that it provides us with a challenge to appreciate the wonder of the gospel *for ourselves* before we start talking about it to other people!

Finally, be reassured: even if you feel that you are weak and inadequate, God can use you in ways that will surprise you!

For further reading

1. Apologetics

On apologetics in general, see:

Corduan, Winfried, *Reasonable Faith: Basic Christian Apologetics* (Nashville, TN: Broadman and Holman, 1994).

Green, Michael, *Evangelism Through the Local Church* (London: Hodder & Stoughton, 1990).

McGrath, Alister E., *Bridge-building: Effective Christian Apologetics* (Leicester: Inter-Varsity Press, 1992). North American edition published as *Intellectuals Don't Need God and Other Modern Myths* (Grand Rapids: Zondervan, 1993).

McGrath, Alister, and Green, Michael, *Springboard for Faith* (London: Hodder & Stoughton, 1993).

Sire, James, *The Universe Next Door*, 2nd edn (Leicester: Inter-Varsity Press, and Downers Grove, IL: InterVarsity Press, 1988).

—, *Discipleship of the Mind: Learning to Love God in the Ways We Think* (Leicester: Inter-Varsity Press, and Downers Grove, IL: InterVarsity Press, 1990).

Classic texts of Christian apologetics which are also worth study include:

Lewis, C. S., *Surprised by Joy* (London: Bles, 1955).

—, *Mere Christianity* (London: Bles, 1952).

Schaeffer, Francis, *The God Who is There* in the *Francis A. Schaeffer Trilogy* (Leicester: Inter-Varsity Press, and Wheaton, IL: Crossway Books, 1990).

2. Specific issues

On the identity and significance of Jesus, including issues relating to the resurrection, see:

Bauckham, R., France, R. T., Maggay, M, Stamoolis, J. and Thiede, C. P., *Jesus 2000: A Major Investigation into History's Most Intriguing Figure* (Oxford: Lion, 1989).

Davis, S. T., *Risen Indeed: Making Sense of the Resurrection* (Grand Rapids: Eerdmans, 1993).

Drane, John, *Jesus and the Four Gospels* (Oxford: Lion, 1984).

France, R. T., *The Evidence for Jesus* (London: Hodder & Stoughton, and Downers Grove, IL: InterVarsity Press, 1987).

Green, Michael, *Who is this Jesus?* (London: Hodder & Stoughton, 1990).

Gumbel, N., *Why Jesus?* (Eastbourne: Kingsway, 1991).

Harris, M. J., *From Grave to Glory: Resurrection in the New Testament* (Grand Rapids: Zondervan, 1990).

Lapide, Pinchas, *The Resurrection of Jesus* (London: SPCK, and Minneapolis: Augsburg, 1983).

McGrath, Alister, *Jesus: Who he is and why he matters* (Leicester: Inter-Varsity Press, 1994).

Morris, L., *Jesus is the Christ* (Grand Rapids: Eerdmans, and Leicester: Inter-Varsity Press, 1989).

Thiede, C. P., *Jesus – Life or Legend?* (Oxford: Lion, 1990).

Wright, N. T., *Who was Jesus?* (London: SPCK, and Grand Rapids: Eerdmans, 1992).

On the nature of salvation, see:

Erickson, Millard J., *Introducing Christian Doctrine* (Grand Rapids: Baker Book House, 1992), pp. 279–325.

Grudem, Wayne, *Systematic Theology: An Introduction to Biblical Doctrine* (Grand Rapids: Zondervan, and Leicester: Inter-Varsity Press, 1994), pp. 657–850.

McGrath, Alister, *Making Sense of the Cross* (Leicester: Inter-Varsity Press, 1992). North American edition published as *What was God Doing on the Cross?* (Grand Rapids: Zondervan, 1993).

Morris, L., *The Apostolic Preaching of the Cross*, 3rd edn (Leicester: Inter-Varsity Press, 1965).

Stott, J. R. W., *The Cross of Christ* (Leicester: Inter-Varsity Press, and Downers Grove, IL: InterVarsity Press, 1986).

On suffering, see:

Brand, Paul, and Yancey, Philip, *Pain: The Gift Nobody Wants* (Grand Rapids: Zondervan, 1993).

Lewis, C. S., *The Problem of Pain* (London: Bles, 1940).

McGrath, Alister, *Suffering* (London: Hodder & Stoughton, 1992).

On the place of women in classical paganism, see:

Arthur, M. B., 'Early Greece: The Origins of the Western Attitude towards Women,' *Arethusa* 6 (1973), pp. 7–58.

Balsdon, J. P. V. D., *Roman Women: Their History and Habits* (London: Bodley Head, 1962).

Pomeroy, Sarah, *Goddesses, Whores, Wives and Slaves* (London: Hale, 1975).

Richter, D. C., 'The Position of Women in Classical Athens,' *Classical Journal* 67 (1971), pp. 1–8.

Tarn, W. W., and Griffith, G. T., *Hellenistic Civilization* (London: Arnold, 1952).

On the place of women in Christianity see:

Brown, Ann, *Apology to Women* (Leicester: Inter-Varsity Press, 1991).

Hayter, Mary, *The New Eve in Christ* (London: SPCK, 1987).

Hooker, Morna, 'Authority on Her Head: An Examination of 1 Corinthians 11:10,' *New Testament Studies* 10 (1964), pp. 410–16.

Mattingley, Harold, *The Man in the Roman Street* (New York: Norton, 1966)

Thomas, W. D., 'The Place of Women in the Church at Philippi,' *Expository Times* 83 (1971), pp. 117–20.

Witherington III, Ben, *Women in the Ministry of Jesus*

(Cambridge: Cambridge University Press, 1984).

—, *Women in the Earliest Churches* (Cambridge: Cambridge University Press, 1988).

An issue of importance which is not fully addressed in this book is the New Age Movement. The following works will be found helpful in exploring this movement, and the challenges it directs against Christianity:

Chandler, Russell, *Understanding the New Age* (Dallas: Word, 1988).

Groothius, Douglas R. , *Unmasking the New Age: Is There a New Religious Movement Trying to Transform Society?* (Leicester: Inter-Varsity Press, 1991; Downers Grove, IL: InterVarsity Press, 1986).

—, *Confronting the New Age: How to Resist a Growing Religious Movement* (Downers Grove, IL: InterVarsity Press, 1988).

—, *Revealing the New Age Jesus: Challenges to Orthodox Views of Christ* (Leicester: Inter-Varsity Press, and Downers Grove, IL: InterVarsity Press, 1990).

Miller, Elliot , *A Crash Course on the New Age Movement: Describing and Evaluating a Growing Social Force* (Grand Rapids: Baker Book House, 1989).

Peters, Ted, *The Cosmic Self: A Penetrating Look at Today's New Age Movements* (San Francisco: Harper, 1991).